SNAKE TALK

Tyson Yunkaporta is an Aboriginal scholar, founder of the Indigenous Knowledge Systems Lab at Deakin University in Melbourne, and author of *Sand Talk* and *Right Story, Wrong Story*. His work focuses on applying Indigenous methods of inquiry to resolve complex issues and explore global crises.

Megan Kelleher belongs to the Barada and Kapalbara peoples of Central Queensland and the branch of the Kelleher clan living in regional Victoria. She is currently undertaking her PhD at RMIT University in the School of Media and Communication, investigating whether the affordances of blockchain technology are culturally appropriate for Indigenous governance.

SNAKE TALK

**TYSON YUNKAPORTA
& MEGAN KELLEHER**

TEXT PUBLISHING MELBOURNE AUSTRALIA

The Text Publishing Company acknowledges the Traditional Owners of the country on which we work, the Wurundjeri people of the Kulin Nation, and pays respect to their Elders past and present.

textpublishing.com.au

The Text Publishing Company
Wurundjeri Country, Level 6, Royal Bank Chambers, 287 Collins Street,
Melbourne Victoria 3000 Australia

Copyright © Tyson Yunkaporta and Megan Kelleher, 2025

The moral rights of Tyson Yunkaporta and Megan Kelleher to be identified as the authors of this work have been asserted.

All rights reserved. Without limiting the rights under copyright above, no part of this publication shall be reproduced, stored in or introduced into a retrieval system, or transmitted in any form or by any means (electronic, mechanical, photocopying, recording or otherwise), without the prior permission of both the copyright owner and the publisher of this book.

First published by The Text Publishing Company, 2025

Cover design by W. H. Chong
Cover photograph by the authors
Page design by Text
Typeset by J&M Typesetting

Printed and bound in Australia by Griffin Press, a member of the Opus Group. The Opus Group is ISO/NZS 14001:2004 Environmental Management System certified.

ISBN: 9781923058460 (paperback)
ISBN: 9781923059412 (ebook)

A catalogue record for this book is available from the National Library of Australia.

 The paper this book is printed on is certified against the Forest Stewardship Council® Standards. Griffin Press holds chain of custody certification SCS-COC-001185. FSC® promotes environmentally responsible, socially beneficial and economically viable management of the world's forests.

For our brothers Hayden and Doomie who are with us always.

CONTENTS

Our Serpent Relations	1
Thus Spake the Snake	18
First Snake	30
Dead Gods, Living Lore	41
Snakes on an Infinite Plane	57
Awe and Law in the Home of the Snake	70
Eve, the Snake Woman	87
Scales, Wings and Crowns	100
Dragons under the Southern Cross	114
Have Snake, Will Travel	129
Deadly Wyrms	140
Serpent Bridges	149
Right Destruction, Wrong Destruction	165
Taniwha Trails	180
Basilisk	191
Illustration credits	213
Acknowledgments	215
What the Snake Says	216

OUR SERPENT RELATIONS

Did you know that the echidna was named after an ancient Greek demon who was half woman and half snake? The European naturalists who christened the species this way encountered an egg-laying mammal with two vaginas and a massive brain, triggering their deepest primal fears of female and reptilian mysteries, personified in a monstrous chimera of western mythology. Woman and snake have always inspired awe in the human imagination, an awe that turned to vengeful wrath the day they stole a piece of fruit from a Middle Eastern garden. After that, things went sideways and men broke the world, smashing the old stories and burying the fragments deep.

Nobody is happy with how all that turned out, and everybody longs to make their culture great again. Perhaps we should do some narrative archaeology to unearth ancient tales that might inspire us to discover a better world together. Not in a scholarly way—it should be an exciting and sexy quest like in the movies, full of heroes and villains, exotic locations and funny (but wise) native guides.

Imagine you are an adventurer, following clues and fighting unscrupulous rivals in a desperate race against Nazis and wealthy super villains to claim the fabled secrets of supreme ancestors, the treasures of legend, to shape the course of history. X marks the spot, encrypted in crumbling papyrus and etched stone, the secret locations of truths and proofs to be preserved, suppressed or weaponised—depending on who gets there first. You unsettle forgotten tombs and lost ruins, seeking answers in the crowns of warrior queens, in the notched bones of giant animals long extinct, in the dusty journals of rogue scholars and bearded mystics. But beware: there be dragons here, and writhing multitudes of hissing creatures lurking in the dark.

Snakes. Why did it have to be snakes?

Beneath your intrepid boots, reptilian mythologies echo from a time before truth, from an age undreamed of, long before the temple-builders, hoarders and ideologues invented vengeful gods to keep their women at home and prevent their teenagers from masturbating. It was an age when we thrived within our biological niche as a custodial species of the land and sea. There's a rustle in the dry grass of history, in this breathless moment before a random lightning bolt or tossed cigarette may set the whole world alight. The old stories, the ones from before the hero's journey began, the half-remembered stuff of ayahuasca trips and nightmares—these take you back to the old ways, and the old ways all have sacred Snakes at their foundation. (It seems appropriate to capitalise the names of the great Serpents as we continue, as people do with all spiritual entities that are held sacred.)

There is no paragon of wisdom who holds all the Serpent knowledge today, but that's okay; nobody knows much about anything alone. Collectively, though, our kin across different tribes carry knowledge about this skin shedder, fast striker, egg-layer, land and water mover—this silent and hidden keeper of secrets.

Basilisk, Wyvern, Naga, Goorialla, Quetzalcoatl and many others connect all this serpentine wisdom across a pluriverse of creation entities, entangling languages, flames, skies, waters and rocks. Let us bring all our stories, fears and fascinations to the campfire and see what we can know, all together in one circle. You can't sit in front of the fireplace, though—only beside it—because there is no wall or chimney and there are people on the other side, so there can be no 'front'. Their faces are distorted by heat and smoke, but so is yours. The view from alongside is the only one that is clear when the fire is too big, so come alongside us. We'll use this Anglo trade dialect we share, making pop culture references from time to time from songs and stories that we may have in common, so we can come into good relation together. Maybe you're not a rugged adventurer after all. You might be happier as a diplomat making cultural embassy, exchanging knowledge with Xhosa, Zhongguoren, Danes, Murris, Nepali, Māori, Celts, Persians and more.

Who do you belong to? Us-two belong to our lands, children, families and each other—an Aboriginal mother and father from Barada and Kapalbara people in Central Queensland and the Apalech clan from Wik Country further north on Western Cape York, entangled with fraught affiliations from Nungar, Pama, Murri and Koori Country, among what our community calls 'Lost Mob'. This means we are bound up with many ancestors and descendants from families beyond our reach and memory, displaced by invaders, seeds scattered tragically but still sprouting fiercely all over, from Palm Island in the north to Kangaroo Island in the south of this continent (which is currently named Australia).

Aunty Munya Andrews, an Elder from the Bardi of Western Australia, told us that the continent used to be called Bandaiyan and that it is the body of a giant ancestor with both male and female genitalia. There are many names and stories, but we don't argue about these things, because we all agree that there are great Serpents running through the living body of this land as threads binding us together in a patchwork quilt of bio-cultural diversity, crisscrossed with ancient ceremonial paths and trade routes. Before the Federation of Australia, this vast Indigenous network extended across the sea in trade with Asia and Melanesia. But the continent has a flag now, and its shores are surrounded and isolated by imaginary lines that we may not cross without a passport.

Protocols of traversing territories and waters for trade, for Ceremony and for embassy still exist for us in the old ways that endure: Sunrise-Sunset Dreaming traditions in which our governance expands in concentric sovereignties from self to pair, to family, to clan, to tribe, to region, to continent and beyond. This is embedded in our languages, with pronouns we translate as I-in-relation, us-two, us-only and us-all. We cannot speak without naming our roles in this relational system of governance. So we're gradually naming these roles and pondering the yet unclear lines of connection that exist between us-two and you-all, stretching across lands and waters and time.

We're comfortable with that uncertainty—in our old protocols of embassy we just let understanding emerge as we share story together. Our thinking-feeling processes take a lot longer than the usual acknowledgements, welcomes, introductions and lessons people expect in modern rituals of knowledge exchange. There are no questions or demands for clarity in our way. If we don't know the difference between Law and Lore, for example, we don't seek a glossary or

Q and A session; we just listen and wait for the context of stories and relationships to shape our understanding.

We are writing this from the lands of the Kulin First Nations in the south-east of the continent, where we have sat patiently for years in these contested territories and stories, slowly coming to understand the Lore of Bunjil—the sacred knowledge of the creator as an eagle, who made the land in partnership with a great Serpent. That Serpent became the Law in the land, which we understand in our traditions as a flow that governs the complexity of right relations in living systems. We respect this deeply, as well as many more stories that seem to contradict each other, but make sense in the overall weave of Lore. Goodithulla (the Barada eagle), a totemic entity in our family, comes alongside Bunjil's Lore, while the Law of the Serpent we honour helps us align with the Law in the lands of Kulin Peoples. In this way we have made kin, worked for community and gained permissions to do our far-reaching thinking, making and Ceremony here.

Data is always incomplete, so good thinking involves feeling through what is revealed when we gather in shared sites of meaning. That's how all human beings learn the inexplicable complexities of culture—through intuitive connection rather than prefabricated information. We've already been way too heavy on the exposition here, so let's get back to the business of sharing the nature of our relationship in the storyscape of Serpents that holds our world together.

OUR SERPENT RELATIONS

As parents and spouses, we're a kin pair, and there is Law for that relation nested in the fabric of creation, carved and woven through Serpent Lore: Thaypan (taipan entity) and Kabul (carpet python entity) entwining ancestral lines sung between sacred sites. They shape the shifting landscape, its signals and essences, and the ngeen wiy, which is the spirit unseen within and all around. They keep regenerative life and death cycles spinning in closed loops of creation and destruction, man and woman, joined across open loops of entropy and sustenance between worlds. One entity's kaka is another entity's lunch. First man, first woman, child. Two snakes. One big story—the reason we don't collapse into a void of non-being.

That old Lore was the dream us-two dreamed the night before our hands first met at a campfire, elliptical orbits of our gendered roles overlapping as man gathers wood and woman keeps the flame. In the dream, we were taller than trees and made of southern lights, walking as the original man and woman did at the birth of the custodial species now called human, by some. But, oh! Dreaming is one thing—colonial reality is another entirely!

In the waking world, a trafficked carpet snake trapped in a terrarium nearby butted its head frantically against the walls of its prison, over and over in the rhythm of our Ceremony, until the glass cracked and the storm that threatened our fire split down the middle and passed on either side of us. From our mother-side and in-law mobs, the old

SNAKE TALK

Kapalbara carpet snake men from the north called out, and we sang back, then—snap!—we woke to the nine-to-five schedules of a world in pain. There is no memory left to us of how that dream ended, only a sense that together we were destined to be more than we had become, that we would do something wonderful to sustain creation, one day.

Life isn't a dream, though, and sublime visions don't put food on the table unless you're leading a cult. A decade later, we wonder if we were mistaken, if perhaps there was no great spiritual destiny for us at all, only dirty nappies, bigotry, violence, bills and grief. Well, maybe it isn't great stories and heroes' journeys that change the world—maybe it's the little things.

Maybe this book is one of those little things.

Our eight-year-old daughter, Onyx, is another little thing we made. She recently asked, 'Did the Rainbow Snake ever fall in love?' She is obsessed with romance, with tales of princes and princesses striving towards a 'happy ever after'. For her, life is still a fairytale, full of magic and sparkling miracles around every corner, just out of sight but beckoning with constant hope and promise. She doesn't like our Dreaming stories very much, because they seldom have happy endings, and love does not conquer all. What facts might we tell her of love? Love is not measurable or verifiable in any way, and there is no objective proof of its existence as a force in the world. We can measure its effects, or the devastating impact of its absence. We can feel love, express love, make love—maybe even buy and sell it—but we can't see it. We can study the wars and murders and great works of art it has inspired and know that it is wonderful and terrible. But as with the awesome and awful Rainbow Serpent, you can't view its components under a microscope, or track its flows with sensors, or capture any evidence that it exists at all.

Although none of the ancient Snake entities from around the world are verifiably real, we feel their Law just as we feel the presence of love, and we believe that the stories humans still tell about them contain some useful wisdom. As our oldest accounts of what creation looked like before walled cities, farms and temples, maybe they can reveal to us how we managed our relationships with the land and all our human and non-human kin over half a million years of life and love.

In a way, mythology is a kind of scientific consensus— reporting on successful behavioural experiments to make laws and protocols, as well as failed ones to share as cautionary tales. We feel like there might be some retrievable data in there, from that long-lost era in which we managed not to wipe ourselves out, knowledge that could be useful during the cataclysmic global phase shift in which we find ourselves.

We have followed the tails of those tales all around the world, seeking the real amidst the scattered debris of the true, in the throats and bellies of knowledge-keepers and in the work of their hands wrought through arts, crafts and sacred objects. We will share some of the knowledge and images of this journey with you.

Did the Rainbow Snake ever fall in love? Yes, bub, he did! He does! There are stories of his romantic dramas all over this land, filled with all the disasters and conflicts that can make love into the most destructive force in the world if it's not handled with care and deep understanding. He leaves those stories with us, so we know how to love in ways that connect each other and all the land, rather than tearing everything apart.

At Rainbow Beach in Queensland, just south of your grandmother's Country, he falls in love with a beautiful woman who is pursued by an evil sorcerer. The wicked man captures her, but the Rainbow Snake rushes in to save her, fighting bravely until he dies of his wounds. His blood stains the sands and to this day you can find every colour of the rainbow on that coastline.

In your grandfather's Country there is a similar story about Thaypan, the Rainbow Serpent, and his wife Thintow, the file snake. She is taken by Wel, the blue-tongue lizard, and Thaypan is killed in battle when he fights to rescue her. Wel eats his heart, and it turns his tongue blue, just like the god Shiva in India when he drinks the venom of the Naga Serpent. The sacred Snake is everywhere in the world, balancing life and death, light and dark, love and hate.

The Rainbow Serpent often dies for love. It's

okay, because he still lives as ngeen wiy, that unseen force within and between things, making big colourful arcs across the sky, and he still moves with the seasons in the water and under the ground. The death of his giant body in those ancient battles was for a reason—to leave Lore for us about right love and wrong love.

Right love is about respecting each other's different ways and protecting them in good relation. It is about finding joy in the freedom and difference of your loved ones. Wrong love is when you want to own, control or possess another person. Wrong love will poison you and all your relationships with people and land. It hurts people so badly that often they can never love the right way again, so they go on to hurt more people. Soon, everyone forgets how to love and starts fighting for power over others, and that's when Rainbow Snake will smack! Wrong love is pretty much the same as hate—you can't stop thinking about a person or a group of people, and you will do absolutely anything to boss and punish them, even if it kills you. That's why we have the Rainbow Snake story, to keep the Lore that tells us how we must behave with the people and land we love.

We say he/him when we tell these stories, because the male entity is the one we are accustomed to in the Lore of our families, but it is important to know that the Serpent also takes female form. There are many stories where the

SNAKE TALK

Rainbow Snake is feminine, and in some places there are rock engravings and paintings that show a male and female together, sometimes with offspring. Often these images also represent the Lore of First Man and First Woman, but it is difficult to translate the logic of this overlap into English print.

In our Lore, entities are transmuted in different times and places, just as songlines shift from one language to the next as you travel across the land and through cycles of time. Songlines are maps, trails storied and sung, where you may be following the steps of a giant man and woman across a plain, but then those mythical footprints become the slide-marks of great bellies when your trail crosses a river and the language changes. It's a bit like when the fella who played Dumbledore in the first Harry Potter films was replaced with a different actor. How did you manage that cognitive dissonance? You probably blinked a couple of times, then shrugged and binged the next movies without any worries.

The networked sovereignties of over five hundred tribes find collective agreement and interdependent governance through a massive diversity of songlines, not through a single dominant narrative. The more pluralistic your Lore is, the more anti-fragile your systems of trade and diplomacy become. Exciting battles will happen from time to time, but devastating wars are impossible. Serpent Lore shows us that boundaries are fluid. Borders are relational spaces-in-between that are dependent on context, rather than permanent defensive barriers to be surveyed and contested. Man–woman, insider–outsider, freshwater–saltwater, mine–yours, self–other—all are dynamic and unified by relational boundaries. Even the boundary between time and space is flexible in this worldview.

That concept is even harder to translate, but in our Indigenous cultures there are usually no separate words for time and place. Suffice to say, *who* you are from moment to moment is bound up with kin, location and trajectory, and *where* you are depends upon *when* you are. The Serpent may be a male shooting lightning from his scales in a particular site and season, but in another place or a different season the same entity can menstruate or lay eggs. They are as mutable as the moon in the sky. They can be mammalian, with bosoms nourishing the land with milk, or crocodilian at another site, and may even have feathers or a huge, shining penis. He may even *be* a penis, sung into Serpent form to trick the unwary. In some places they have horns on their head—the Serpents, not the penises (how weird would that be?). But it's all pretty weird, because no horned creatures existed on this continent until two centuries ago, so how on earth did that feature come into the stories? In all their fabulous and diverse forms, our Serpents remind us not to get too attached to binaries.

When we authentically follow our old ways, we are comfortable with boundaries being dynamic across different systems, territories and categories—even genders. We hold sacred many totemic species of protandrous hermaphrodites, such as barramundi fish, for example, so we understand that all things have stages and cycles of change, dancing in spectrums of variety and complexity. Old men grow breasts, and old women grow beards. The Serpent is a rainbow with many colours, which you can see when water hits the air just right. They're not always so motley, though—sometimes they can even be white, like the Mundagatta on Murruwarri Country in the season when the water level rises in the river. So we're quite inclusive when it comes to interacting with others different from ourselves.

Traditionally, in theory, at least. Well, the world is complicated, you know? No generalities work anymore in this post-truth world! (Unless they're lies, of course.)

We speak from an amazing, ancient, ingenious culture, but it's not the same as it was two centuries ago. There is continuity and discontinuity. Past and present are domains with fluid boundaries, just like everything else.

Most of our families have spent a few generations in church. It was either that or get shot, and we did our best, but the Lore has shifted quite a bit. Don't judge us too harshly for this. We'll forgive the shooting, if you can forgive us for all the things we gave up at gunpoint. That's the spirit of reconciliation! Borders as fluid spaces of kin-making are great until people who don't get that concept move in next door and burn your house down, with you in it. Is that one of those situations where we're supposed to love the sinner and hate the sin?

Anyway, Jesus is totally Lord and Saviour, and we're comfortable with any cognitive dissonance around that declaration, along with all the fleets of contradictory stories that are now woven into our Lore and protocols today. Our house is a jumble of competing values—one of us is a devout monotheist and the other is a heathen and part-time sceptical atheist—but we can still manage to raise neurodivergent kids and write a book together. A senior Law Man we both admire (who was both a cultural adept and a Christian minister) once said that a lot of holy writ is evil, but the gospel is good story. We can work with that around our chaotic kitchen table.

Monotheism from the Global North, however, has brought competition, superiority and exclusion to our shores and into the hearts of our people. It has introduced some troubling ideas about the Serpent as an 'ancient enemy', a representation of evil and sin to be purged from our flawed inner selves and from a world infested with inferior pagans and heretics. Amidst all the theft and genocide of colonisation, the missionaries and zealots charged with civilising us justified, normalised and even celebrated boundary violation as a way of life, and that changed everything for us. Now, many of us squabble over property, morality and identity, and shun our gay kids, the same as everyone else. Just like you, we have experienced the depredations of development enforced by corrupt hierarchies wielding the power of a wrathful god of vengeance. But that started long ago in a far-off land, millennia before a fella called Abraham found himself with a really shitty choice to make, way back when most of our ancestors were still doing okay.

In Persia, Serpent Law gave way to the coercive doctrines of religious sects, then conflict among the many cults gave bloody birth to the image of an exclusive lord of all creation, inspiring new stories of dominance and supremacy over outsiders, and even over nature itself. In those strange tales, the one who kills the giant reptile is the hero, not the villain. The myth of divine slayers spread and husbanded a dominion of monotheistic seeds, sprouting from the corpses of Dragons, spawning cities and cultures of conquest. When it arrived here a couple of centuries ago, that perfected narrative of supremacy introduced a system of boundaries and sovereignties that destroyed good relations between peoples, lands, generations and genders.

So now we sing songs of praise while fighting over revised histories and claims to territories both real and imagined, and some of us manage to navigate a path of integrity through the hostile terrain of competing colonial imaginaries. Most of us don't. We fight our way through elections, holidays, workplace coups and family meals, shouting our preferred truths about what is really normal and ignoring what is normally real. Folklores and paper laws are manipulable, while the sacred is reduced to whatever serves our agendas from moment to moment.

We know that humans are better than this. So we're going back to where all this mess started, to wander through the ruins and seek the wisdom of those who yet carry the memories of long ago, when a world that was still guided by the spirit of the Serpent suddenly turned around and started eating itself.

THUS SPAKE THE SNAKE

This chapter tells the stories of a Serpent spirit that is pure evil and malice. It will ruin things for people seeking solace in the false binaries and appeals to ancient wisdom offered by so many grifters in today's marketplace of ideas. We want to build gradually to a sense of hope and shared reality in this book, so we're putting this yarn near the start, where the mood is still a little damp and dark before the sunrise and rainbows appear. We do believe that there is compatible Lore around the world in the fragments of Serpent stories that remain from the ages before monotheism, but we're not going to pretend that every mythic reptile is a paragon of peace, love and mindfulness. With Snakes, you never know what you're going to get. They're a bit like people, in that way—some of them bite and it bloody hurts.

Our deep-time stories in Indigenous Australia have always warned us about the folly of doomed communities experimenting with power systems built on necrotic mythologies that banish the Serpent. Invariably, something terrible would always move in the land or the sky, wiping those experiments from the face of the Earth and leaving us with cautionary tales about the horrors of coercive hierarchies and insatiable extraction. Perhaps our cousins far across the sea understood this for a very long time too, before things changed when the oceans rose and drowned many lands, triggering a plethora of biological and cultural adaptations across the globe. This was a relatively recent development, around ten thousand years ago, and while we managed our changing coastline and drying continent here, an aberration was occurring in distant places unknown to us. It was a cultural anomaly that gave rise to the concept of linear time, so we are using past tense for this part of our Serpent journey to mark that shift in human consciousness. Traditionally, we tell our Lore stories in present tense because the past is continually unfolding in the present, but that temporal orientation doesn't seem to work in our encounters with Zoroastrian Serpent tales.

After the last ice age ended, a singular and all-powerful god called Ahura Mazda arose in the Middle Eastern region that would become known as 'the fertile crescent', declaring universal supremacy and claiming credit for creating the entire universe. His followers denied the existence of other creation entities, while simultaneously calling for their eradication. Many of these rival entities were depicted as long and reptilian, and demi-god agents of the supreme being were sent on quests to destroy them all. A pluriverse of intersubjective realities was consumed in an eternal war for the dominance of one myth, one creator. Communities and cultures were overtaken by narrative and kinetic violence on a scale never seen before, holy wars between the children of light and darkness to establish the dominion of the righteous (like US politics but with swords and sandals).

Dragons were slain, Snakes were crushed beneath heels and mythical holy warriors (who would later inspire St George and St Patrick) eventually vanquished the pagan beasts to sit in splendid dominion, awaiting the death and ascendance of their deity and his prophets. They hoped that death would trigger a great reset of creation and glorious resurrection to heal the suffering of the extractive power systems they created, but instead it brought forth constant revolution with increasingly harsh biological feedback, smashing their lives at each new turn of the wheel. *Next time, next time*, they prayed, *there will be a return, and there will be no more death*. The desertification that always afflicts civilisations with growth-based economies exacerbated the problem of water scarcity, and the ancient kings blamed the Dragons for it.

THUS SPAKE THE SNAKE

Our good friend Sousan Abadian, a Zoroastrian Indigenous scholar we met in Indiana at a symposium of theologians from around the world, shared some Dragon stories with us. She told us that the great Serpents at that time represented evil and disorder, and that the epic heroes of Persian mythology often slayed them, as depicted in the *Shahnameh* (Epic of Zoroastrian Kings). This text is important today in Iran, as it has allowed the people to recover and retain their traditional language despite multiple invasions and the spread of Arabic as the dominant tongue in the region. One of the heroes in this sacred text is named Rostam, who Sousan told us would later become the inspiration behind the Christian story of St George slaying the Dragon.

Rostam is known as a *negahban*, a protector of Iran's monarchy, particularly of weak, corrupt or ineffective kings who need divine help to stay in power. During his quest to rescue one of these rich brat despots from demons, Rostam became tired and fell asleep, unaware of a massive, eighty-metre-long Dragon stalking him. His horse disturbed Rostam's sleep to warn him of the danger several times, but the Dragon made itself invisible every time he woke, until in frustration the hero threatened to cut off his horse's legs if it happened again. Eventually the one-and-only god, Ahura Mazda, had to reveal the Dragon to Rostam, because the horse was just as afraid of its rider as it was of the hungry Dragon.

SNAKE TALK

In the end, the faithful steed saved the hero's life by biting the Dragon on the neck, giving Rostam the opportunity to cut off its head. This was the third of seven trials for the hero, at the completion of which he restored the feckless king to power and the Persian empire continued to expand. It is possible that Rostam continued mistreating animals without consequence. It is also possible that his horse taught him a valuable lesson about making kin with animals, but the story doesn't mention it. We like to think the message is implied.

Our yarns with Sousan led us to reflect on the problem of empires—that the mechanism of their power is also the source of their inevitable decline and fall. The aggressive and exclusionary borderwork that makes a civilisation mighty also makes its cultural boundaries difficult to police, so the more alienated people you displace and absorb to keep the kingdom growing, the more foreign influence corrupts your centres of power. We explored this idea further with Nargues Teimoury, an Iranian scholar who told us about how cultural influence from the Silk Road trade during the Mongol occupation came to transform the region's relationship with Serpent spirit over time.

Nargues is originally from Mashhad in the northeast of Iran, and now lives in Isfahan. We spoke with her while she was studying the cultural impacts of the Ilkhani period in the thirteenth century, when Mongol invaders, who had converted to Buddhism, ruled for two hundred years, before gradually converting to Islam and departing as their empire collapsed. Exposed to benevolent Serpent entities like Loongs and Nagas through Buddhist rule and Silk Road trade, Persians developed less inimical relations with Snake spirits for a time. The supply chains and trade routes of empire had an influence on Zoroastrian and Abrahamic conceptions of Serpent entities, which can be seen in the art, craft and architecture of the period.

Traditionally, Persians never depicted Serpents, as they were an image of evil that brought bad luck, but in the time of Mongol rule Dragon and Snake motifs proliferated in stone buildings and sculptures, as well as everyday craft items like jewellery and pottery. Many of these artifacts still remain, but Serpent motifs in modern craft items are rare. After the Mongol rulers departed, Persians returned to an avoidance relationship with the Dragon, known in the ancient texts as Azhdaha.

Nargues told us that Dragons in her tradition are gigantic snake-like creatures with wings, originally the enemies of Tishtrya, the god of rain, who was part of a polytheistic pantheon that existed before Zoroastrianism. Water was sacred in this dry region, and the winged Azhdaha was an entity of dryness that prevented rainfall and blocked the flow of rivers, so had to be hunted and destroyed by heroes to release water for the people.

Persian Dragons are not beings of fire, air and water as in other traditions. They are evil beings of dryness that suppress these sacred elements, although they did play a role in the human discovery of fire, which is still celebrated at the end of each year during the Feast of Sada. As Nargues tells it, the story describes a great hero throwing a giant boulder at a Dragon but missing it completely. The missile collided with a different kind of rock, producing sparks that ignited the world's first fire.

She told us a few stories that began with a Dragon preventing rainfall or river flows to deprive a city of its water supply. One story was about Rostam's grandfather slaying a giant Dragon that was lying across the Karkheh River, resulting in a drought and the death of many cattle. Today, a dam wall lies across the river to block its flow. While the dam provides water for the city, its depletion of the river causes catastrophic dust storms in the region, and we wonder how the Iranians make sense of that. Do they think of the dam wall as an evil Azhdaha or as a benevolent bringer of water and life? In our Aboriginal way of thinking, the river flow is facilitated by the Serpent who also brings rain, so it is hard to make sense of this paradox. We were too polite to ask Nargues about it, though, because we had only just met her.

Instead we asked her if there was any provocation for the Dragon's behaviour. In our stories the Serpent usually goes into destruction mode because the people have been doing something wrong in land care, governance or Ceremony, and are in need of correction. Nargues said no: that is just the nature of Dragons, as entities representing 'very bad things'. In solar and lunar eclipses, a Dragon is said to be eating the sun or moon, and still today in Iran the people stand on their rooftops during eclipses, banging metal objects to frighten the beast away. In every aspect, Nargues informed us, Persian Dragons are pure evil, with no agenda other than to do harm to people and the land.

She added that they are also a symbol of bad spirit within yourself, the evil that you must struggle with daily to become a better person. This is why they were not traditionally depicted before Persian connection with the Silk Road, because their images bring ill luck that disrupts personal development. It must have been extremely disturbing when Mongols started carving Dragons on the walls of palace buildings and temples, but gradually the people came to respect these carved stone images, which still adorn buildings and statues in Iran today, albeit in uneasy relation with Zoroastrian and Islamic art and architecture.

A significant Islamic Serpent motif in Iran depicts an ancient king with a Snake on each shoulder. He used to kill two young men each day to feed them. That story is about Iran's first revolution, in which the people revolted against the tyrant and imprisoned him for two thousand years. But, as with Zoroastrian traditions, in Islam the greatest struggle is not in war and politics, but within the self, in every human's quest to conquer their own worst impulses. Even as a symbol of pure evil, the Serpent still guides us towards balance and harmony. As Nargues says, without the

Azhdaha there can be no enlightenment, because if there is no beast there can be no struggle within to conquer the evil of one's own heart and become a hero. How can you be a hero if there is nothing to slay?

Nargues told us that in Zoroastrianism one can conquer the evil within by following the example set by the hero ancestors in their epic battles with dragons. One must follow a three-fold path similar to that of Buddhism—good speech, good thought and good deeds. Mastery of these principles in daily life is represented by the symbol of the *faravahar*, which signifies the flying spirit of a person who has won the internal battle with evil and is ready to become a hero who may wage war against the external evils of the world.

Dragon-slaying is only one stage in the hero's journey. There are seven trials, some of which seem to be aligned with the mundane challenges all colonised peoples face: enduring scarcity, suppressing sexuality, working hard in the service of ruling elites and struggling against white devils. (Jokes! Just jokes!) The white devil is the final trial. Nargues said we don't have to contend with the black devil of chaos and darkness, because that one was an entity from ancient times who was conquered by Ahura Mazda when he became the one-and-only god. The white devil is more about physical might and kinetic warfare, originally inspired by light-skinned invaders from the north who were eventually expelled. Everybody likes to invade Iran from time to time, but nobody can ever hold it for long.

Nargues asserts that even after the Mongol invaders left Persia, invasions and colonisation continued through commerce, because the Silk Road remained as a mechanism of extraction that drained their resources for centuries. 'We are still in the middle of the Silk Road,' she said, 'and since the nineteenth century we have oil, and this oil brought things back to us. Not all good things. When you have oil, you have struggle inside and you have struggle outside.'

She reflected that oil is buried treasure and that the twelfth century Iranian Dragons emerging from Chinese cultural influence were mythological guardians of treasure, resting uneasily in the collective imagination as continued commerce and extraction added contradictory layers to the people's relationship with Serpent spirit. Centuries later, courtesy of Anglo oil interests in the region, fundamentalist regimes installed by foreign powers altered traditional governance systems forever, enriching some with jealously guarded treasure, while impoverishing multitudes. In spite of this, the common people of Iran do not see oil in their everyday lives. As Nargues told us, 'The people pay more attention to water than oil. The oil is for the government, not for the people, so it's not related to the culture and folklore.' The old ways endure; water is still the most precious and sacred substance, and the Dragons are still primal entities of dryness that threaten this holy element.

In the spirit of embassy, we shared stories with Nargues of our own drought-making monsters. In our family's tradition it is not a Serpent who holds back the water, but an echidna. However, the most famous drought monster in Aboriginal Australia is a frog called Tiddalik, so we mostly focused on that one. In that story, the giant amphibian entity drinks all the water in the land and keeps it for himself, so the other animals must trick him into putting it all back. He's a greedy bugger and it's not an easy task, but eventually they make him laugh until he vomits, and the water is returned.

We have a lot of stories from a time when the land became dry, legends of giant megafauna that had to be downsized so that a greater diversity of animals no larger than kangaroos could take their place. This meant that the biological niches of massive beasts like diprotodons could be occupied by many herbivores grazing an extended menu of less thirsty plants, creating abundance for all in a new age of water scarcity. Serpent manages the flow of precious water, moving it around seasonally so that everybody gets some when they need it (unless dams and extractive irrigation get in the way). Every landscape is also a storyscape filled with knowledge, and narrative maps of Lore spread like networks of veins from the paths made by sacred flows of water and giant Snakes.

This is something all Serpent Lore has in common, even in cultures as vastly different as Zoroastrian Persia and Aboriginal Australia—our first duty as a custodial species is to revere and care for waterways. Whether our Snakes are good or evil, they all remind us of that prime directive. We also hold in common the notion that Serpent spirit always moves us through times of change and upheaval, guiding us in our struggles to maintain balance and order in society and nature.

Nargues said that mystical struggles with Serpent spirit drove ancient construction projects creating irrigation systems in the fertile crescent that remain in use today, so deep that the Eiffel Tower could easily be immersed in them. Their Azhdaha have always inspired great feats in the preservation of life and land. They hide in the mountains and the forests that surround them, lurking by the sources of rivers there, waiting for cycles of change and upheaval. Her people understand, as folks all around the world do, that when they emerge we must pay attention and alter our behaviour.

There are signs and signals of change in our own lands now, so we step out of the timeline of history and return to present tense (and a tense present). We are called home for Ceremony, to make sense of warnings and crisis, grounding ourselves in our Serpent Lore and the Law of the land before we can continue our journey together.

FIRST SNAKE

There have been nightmares surging in our circles of Ceremony lately, hard visions of snakes thrashing in a warped reality where we give-give while others take-take and we all fall forward in an unstoppable rush towards catastrophe. There is a distortion in creation, with rainbow and lightning and fire moving the waters strangely. In a recent saltwater Ceremony at sunrise, four whales breached and sprayed mist through the light, forming twisted rainbows as dolphins surfed towards the dawn ritual with messages of strife. Alarm and frustration signals sound in the tangled lines of images painted and songs sung. It is a time of dry spells, but also torrents of water hitting the earth with power and fury, the Serpent's head coming back around to bite, demanding we meet our obligations to waterways in the land, sea and sky.

Narratives old and new give us validation and caution, as natural justice cuts both ways. We share stories of the two sides that Serpent spirit shows in Law, as pairs of long-spined beings moving from east to west, or as a swirling dyad of creation and destruction contained in one entity. The entities can take the form of eel-like, crocodile-like or snake-like beings, but they all evoke an ancient push-pull between opposing forces seeking balance.

We recently travelled to the Bunya Mountains, a sacred place in southern Queensland, for a week of kin-making and Ceremony. There are mimburi there, sites of flow and increase that keep creation from collapsing into entropy, because every system in the universe leaks energy and must be topped up from somewhere. These spiritual sites of flow don't function unless we are working with them in Ceremony, which is one of our most important roles as a custodial species. No Ceremony, no increase; no increase, no living systems. Increase is different from growth—it's not about size and number, but diversity and connections. The land is a network of signals activated through a multitude of interconnected cycles, like the cogs inside a watch, and Ceremony is at the centre of it all.

Every seasonal scent, display of colour, movement,

behaviour, migration, secretion, weather change, fight, mating dance, death, birth and each tiny sound triggers a response and a new phase of behaviour for other beings and phenomena in the living system. Our Ceremonies and rituals are in the rhythm of these cycles: daily, yearly and in rotations of deep-time calendars in the night sky. The ritual sounds and movements we make are signals that our non-human kin perceive, triggering reactions that have become part of the evolutionary weave of our ecosystems.

We can design rituals to alter the signals in different times and places in response to change that needs to be managed, and the butterfly effects of these innovations across interconnected regions near and far are understood and calculated from the connective informatics of Serpent Law (not Butterfly Law—that is for something else). So we must travel every few years for multi-tribal Ceremonies in particularly powerful sites to make sense of the complexities of managing networks of bioregions connected by weather flows and migration over vast distances. The Serpent has left songlines for us to travel for this purpose.

This is Indigenous embassy and, in the gathering place of the Bunya Mountains, it is a tree that sets the schedule and calls in the people for the right ceremonial moment in the right ritual cycle. Bunya pines existed long before the first grasses appeared on the earth, so they are old enough to know what they are doing. Dinosaurs with long, serpentine necks used to rely on them as a food source, and the cataclysm that wiped out those mighty reptiles failed to eradicate these elders of the plant world. They have adapted through uncountable armageddons of climate change and meteor strikes and volcanic eruptions. Their massive pine nuts are too much for any bird to carry, so they are only spread by humans in this age and they have formed a special relationship with us. When they grow away from their home in southern Queensland, they take on different shapes as ambassadors adjusting to diverse bio-cultures—we saw one in Tasmania once, and barely recognised it.

On their home ground, they take their true form and their cycles are like clockwork, signalling a three-year ritual rotation for peak abundance and Ceremony. The bunya nuts are only large and fat every third year, to signal the provisioning of visitors from far-off lands who gather in the mountains in vast numbers to feast and make embassy. This has been happening there for as long as humans can remember, in places made sacred by a giant carpet python entity called Kabul, who is a creation being far older than any tree.

An important part of Ceremony in that part of the world is wanjau, which roughly translates to 'collective sense-making'. This is a form of yarning that requires high levels of cultural knowledge, relational capacity and cognitive complexity. It is ongoing, and its ideas are carried away with the bunya nuts to seed knowledge production in all directions. The wanjau we are sharing here is part of an ongoing series of yarns in that bunya rhythm and following the protocols of Kabul's Law.

So before we share more Serpent stories of many cultural adepts from around the world, we will set circle here by translating some of this wanjau, from a collective of Aboriginal thinkers, from Cobble Cobble, Gumbayngiir, Bandjalang, Wik, D'harawal and Gamilaraay tribes, who begin by grounding us in continental common Law and the Serpent Lore we all share in embassy.

Our songman sings us in as Kabul is moving in seasonal Ceremony through mimburi, his ritual increase sites hyperconnected far and wide from the Bunyas. Our voices in response are inflected with the spirit of diverse tongues, places, names and images of that carpet snake entity, calling, Cobble, Gapal, Kapool, Gabul-gabul, Gubulla, Jumbal, Ooyngorpan, in storied paths that fork or join, depending on which way you are walking. Gumbayngiir connects along the coast, and Gamilaraay comes through the Western Bunya Mountains along corridors of Ceremony and trade. Brolga and carpet snake find totemic relations in the far north. There are old and new family stories from millennia and decades ago, all planted in the deep time of Ceremony. Our languages mingle, with words from our diverse tongues studded throughout the Kriolised English we are using. Each speaker is a living nexus of time–place relationships, voicing traditional connections and new stirrings of disturbing Serpent dreams and encounters that show us the time and place are finally right for this work.

Underground water is surging seasonally, linking to the movement of Mundagatta, Waawey and Garriya Serpent beings from the west, bringing blessings but also warnings for our children to avoid rising waters. H_2O is gentle, until it is not. We are reminded to balance flame and liquid as elements in Ceremony and in the land-care activity that comes from this ritual activity, ensuring our disturbances of natural systems are maintained as regenerative actions. We affirm that even our waste is a sacred essence in this storyscape, with the guna of the Serpent leaving geological features as reminders to respect our secretions, and to warn us not to shit where we drink. As always in these deep Serpent Lore yarns, the storytellers need to take jilliwa breaks with unusual frequency as the waters move in story through our bodies. Even ocham (urine) is a totemic substance—everything is sacred for somebody.

In our wanjau, we agree that the sacred and the profane are two sides of the same coin, and we remind each other that the putrid by-products of our daily living must be deposited with care to nourish cycles of increase in creation. We speak of the waters in our bodies expressing the lifeblood flows of the land—the sweat of our physical effort moves with the waters of land and climate, and our tears ebb and flow with emotion to show us how to align our social behaviours and governance with biological structures. When our physical and mental labours are grounded in these things, we produce spiritual energy that joins the flow of the Law, which then feeds back through us. All this is shaped by multidimensional patterns and principles, above and below the ground as well as within us. Our rituals here follow Serpent activity and cycles, activating desire lines we intuit together as pathways over time, flowing gently when we walk with attention to signals from land and trends in culture and trade.

It all changes when things are out of balance, though. Our Ceremony in one sacred site is disturbed by 'Fuck You!' graffiti sprayed on the rock, the initials of settlers carved into the stone eye of the Serpent, Scottish thistles spiking our children's feet while tourists dive over the waterfall and have sex in the pond. We would like to make a fire, but we would be fined or worse for doing that, in this place that has been designated as a nature preserve and recreation facility.

The power systems of global economies are pulling us out of the life-giving loops and spirals that move our species as custodians, perverting the spirit of collective knowledge and fencing us, boxing us into isolationist stories by design. Our old Lore tells us that the Serpent shifts into destruction mode in such periods, resetting systems catastrophically to restore harmony. If the stories are forgotten and mistakes repeated, the cycles of destruction become harsher each time around.

None of us minds whether this story is regarded as literal or metaphorical by anybody choosing to sit around our fires and listen to our wanjau. Either way, our people have found that the knowledge in our stories can provide accurate models for predicting change, and tools for managing change at scale. More importantly, it provides mature understandings of mortality and purpose, which help us avoid the fear that feeds lawless behaviour and mass extinction events. As a diagnostic tool, it can reveal the pathologies of young cultures with unhealthy beliefs about mortality and offer methods of storytelling and inquiry to heal this spiritual affliction.

We arrive at the conclusion that the originating seed of unhealthy cultures is usually a mythology of departed gods, like distant fathers who went out for a pack of cigarettes and never came home. If you personify creation in a powerful entity that can be destroyed by evil unless it is enclosed in a different realm, then your understanding of environmental and social care is going to be flawed. Every ideology, no matter how secular, is the branch of a tree grown from superstition. If the root of that tree is a god of mass murder, end times and escape to another world, then you will never find a rational way to manage your social behaviour in alignment with your biology. Moreover, you will never maintain crucial principles of adaptation and continuity during massive phase shifts. As our Elders say, if you don't move with the land, then the land will move you.

When species go extinct in times of climate transition, our Aboriginal cultures do not think of them as deceased totemic entities. Their forms are kept in the geology of place, and still hold the Law for their ecological niche, which informs the behaviour and management of the new species that evolve or are introduced to replace them. The thylacine (or Tasmanian tiger) is not gone, even on the mainland where it became extinct thousands of years ago. He keeps the story and behavioural patterns of the seasons, stars and uncountable forces combined within quoll, dog and dingo Law, and in the natural systems that emerged and found equilibrium following his demise.

For example, Akngwelye is the name of a giant stone thylacine who guards the entrance to Alice Springs in central Australia. Humans are supposed to stop and seek his permission before entering, a bit like the Sphinx in Greek mythology, but most drive past without knowing his story. So we still sing thylacine songs in new and old forms, maintaining the continuity of his ecologies across deep-time transitions between eras of upheaval and change. He is known in the Lore as a companion of the Rainbow Serpent, and they are even depicted side by side in rock art, so his extinction is not the end of a line; for the Serpent, moments of death are specks in a timeless field of potentialities. Daunting concepts like extinction, loss and change are not limited by modern connotations of traumatic finality in this deep-time understanding of creation, which shapes our thinking as we work to bring new species and cultures into better relationship with the land. One day we hope to have Lore even for feral foxes, so they can come into balance with

FIRST SNAKE

this land too—we're hoping the Irish Lore-keepers we're working with will help us out with that.

Our circle of thinkers shares stories of the great Serpent murdered or killed in battle throughout a pluriverse of existence. He dies on a beach defending a woman and bleeds colours into the sand; he is ambushed on a ridge and cut to pieces; he is killed by a water rat in a lake—yet still he abides in this realm in myriad forms. Death does not transport his spirit elsewhere. We know this is a story held by many cultures around the world—such as Quetzalcoatl in South America, a feathered serpent who passed centuries ago but still exists in the Lore of communities that care for land and village in the patterns of his being. Snake is everywhere, but he is neither dead nor alive and you can't pray to him. You can only commune with him in your careful treatment of water, and his many deaths will not prevent him from turning on you if you fail to respect your sacred role in caring for those flows in concert with clean fire, air, light and earth. Young societies grown from death cults don't understand this, and thus every age of transition now becomes an age of extinction.

In our wanjau we express the need for protection of our knowledge when speaking of the Serpent outside of our circle. In sharing story with others who have no Law, we must be mindful of the colonising action of these young imperial cults, and their insatiable hunger for Indigenous Knowledge (IK) and Traditional Ecological Knowledge

(TEK). It is gathered and stored in stasis, with secular and spiritual inquiry both deeply informed by stories of dead gods and all-powerful lords, driving the imperative to kill the sacred and eradicate the spirit of knowledge. Once it is made inanimate, it can be mined like rocks for inspiration and comfort during the final decades of human existence, or for tinkering the technological ascendence and immortality of a worthy few. If we are gathering a world of stories around one fire here, we need to include the young and old because they are all to be respected, but we also can't allow them to destroy each other. That's our ethical boundary in this work.

In all the stories of creation and destruction around the world, we find that the spirit of the Serpent has endured. Even as a symbol of evil and sin, the deep mythos of our species has retained the core principles of balance at the heart of the ancient knowledge that binds us. The struggle against the Serpent is internalised as a cosmic and eternal drama between fire and water, lust and care, light and murk, bending the arc of history towards periods of balance. Our protocols of embassy in the Bunya Mountains force us to acknowledge that there are a billion eyes on the Snake, which makes for an ambivalent lens when trying to assert values from an individual viewpoint. When we peer at the world through that multifaceted view, the image is distorted if you don't have spirit-grounded protocols for sharing what you see with others and respecting what they share with you in turn.

DEAD GODS, LIVING LORE

Quetzalcoatl is a puzzling expression of Serpent spirit, if you are meeting him from the perspective of a hunter-gatherer culture. He belongs to an Indigenous tradition, but it is an urban, agricultural and sedentary one, an ancient system of civilisation and development in Central America and the south-western United States. Despite his preferred pronouns, he is known as a being of balance between masculine and feminine, earth and sky, serpent and bird. He embodies the ritual knowledge of regenerative agriculture—such as 'the sisters', the trinity of corn, beans and squash as optimal companion plants—both in the soil and in the gut. He is a god of advanced achievements in science and fine arts, as well as being a custodian of nature who carries a bag of copal (aromatic resin) to burn as incense in the ritual blessing of the Four Winds.

We wonder how much the transition of the Toltecs from hunter-gatherers to city-builders (and, eventually, survivors of Spanish colonisation) impacted Serpent spirit. We are interested to know whether Quetzalcoatl's passing integrated him into the living landscape (as occurs in our Indigenous cultures), or whether he enjoyed a more civilised ascension to fantastic realms far removed, with greater cosmic power but less capacity for physical intervention on earth, like Jesus or Yoda. Our Serpent Law makes it hard for us to think in such binaries, though, so our curiosity is redirected towards the possibility that both ways might exist at once, that there could be unique secrets in Toltec Lore for embedding the large-scale interventions of civilisation more harmoniously in sacred landscapes without triggering extinction-level events.

Civilisation is hard to define. All cultures can be called civilised, if you go by the check list of arts practice, engineering, knowledge proliferation, bread-making, and land management for food production. The debate about who can claim a civilised identity is part of a vicious culture war in Australia, divided along the usual partisan lines of settler politics as they fight about whether First Peoples should be thrown into the fire of modernity or melted in the pot of post-modernity. Yes, we were making bread tens of thousands of years before the Egyptians did, and we had many large-scale engineering projects, trade networks and food production systems, but the purpose and logic of using those examples to claim civilised status is unclear to us. It is a bit like holding up a jar of onion jam as proof that root vegetables can be classified as fruit.

As far as we can tell, civilisations are distinguished from other cultures by the genetic modification of grains for intensified production at scale to feed sedentary settlements that are continuously expanding. Even if they are not aggressively increasing their borders, civilisations displace species to make room for intensive agriculture. People live separately from these cultivated areas, allowing ecological niches for foragers to remain unoccupied between harvests. Vacant niches are attractors in natural systems, so nearby animal and insect populations are drawn to those areas to re-establish biodiversity and balance, vacating places further afield to do so. Then they encounter the murderous machine of civilised borderwork.

Those policing the borders resist the flow of biological migration, eradicating all intruders to protect their families and crops, but in doing so they increase the ecological vacuum that continues to draw species from niches far beyond the settlement. Even greater numbers are then attracted to these spiralling vacancies, until a kind of biological black hole is created, with the city at its centre, sucking all life towards a terminal vortex. For the poor bastards charged with policing the frontier, this irresistible rush creates the perception of a wild and chaotic nature teeming with hordes of marauding beasts, spawning new narratives and nightmare imaginaries of demonic invaders, primal enemies of order.

Economies emerge from these stories of competition and survival, control systems that mirror the death spiral pattern that grips the land, creating empires of extraction to suck natural resources from the territories of vanquished neighbours. These human kin can either die miserably in degraded homelands or succumb to the vortex and face the ordeals of border crossing and ghetto life. Cultural and spiritual black holes are also formed in response to the bio-economic whirlpool of city-building. They consume sacred sites of increase and the Serpents who protect them, along with the people of the land who care for those places and entities.

All of this, from a bit of Bronze Age GMO corn!

Quetzalcoatl offers us a tantalising proposition amidst the insatiable vortices consuming our world—what if the spiral could be reversed? Thought experiment: if a disrupted spiritual niche is filled by an entity of balance and respect for nature, then can the black hole of a permanent settlement be stabilised and embedded sustainably in a healthy landscape?

But where has Quetzacoatl gone? We're concerned to find out if he is dead or alive now.

Perhaps our curiosity about him is simply the force of

attraction exerted by the void of his passing from the world, and we are being sucked into a swirl of cosmic annihilation. Or maybe he remains in the Law and Ceremony of the living land and its people, like our own Serpent beings on this continent, calling us to make kin with Mesoamericans and sit together in embassy to share knowledge. We hope it is the latter, rather than the former. It's one thing for a made-up creation entity to be obliterated, but if a real one disappeared completely, the singularity of that event would be unimaginable.

We can't hear even a faint whisper of his voice in historical and anthropological writings about the Toltec Empire, or in the poorly translated fragments of hieroglyphs. The only way to explore propositions like this, to ponder old ways for our salvation in the present, is to speak to keepers of knowledge who continue to inhabit their ancestral landscapes of meaning, even long after their sacred sites and sovereignties have been decimated. The Law of the land is stubborn like that. So our friend Kevin Murray (editor of *Garland Magazine*) introduces us to Eduardo Aguilar Zarandona, a Mesoamerican thinker and scholar from a family that keeps the old Serpent Law in song, dance, daily ritual and art. By video link, he shares with us some stories and wisdom from their winged deity, a being who may have once solved the sustainability problems of civilisation (except for those involving bad guests and psychotic visitors, of course).

SNAKE TALK

Eduardo comes to us fresh from Ceremony the previous day, a twenty-four-hour marathon of Indigenous dance that has not depleted him, but filled him with energy. This is a point of connection with us, as we share an understanding of the power of ritual increase, whereby spirit flows through sacred processes and energises everybody and everything in the landscape, holding the inevitable decay of creation at bay and stabilising living systems. We also recognise the seasonal rain patterns he describes in his land, similar to the climate of north Queensland—a year divided into two halves of wet and dry. He speaks of this duality in the same way we do, not as opposites but as complementary aspects of an indivisible whole. Quetzalcoatl embodies this logic as a unity of male and female, earth and sky, light and dark, snake and bird, material and spirit, city and nature.

When Eduardo says the name Quetzalcoatl it sounds right, but when we say it our mouths just can't form the right shape. We would have to live in Mexico for a while, waiting for the land to shape our tongues the right way, if we wanted to call out for him there. AI has trouble with the name too, replacing it with strange English phrases in our transcripts. *Kids' Soccer. Cancel God. Kiss the Court. Capsule Cockle. Kettle Corn.*

Corn is where Eduardo's Quetzalcoatl story begins. He says the Olmecs and other Indigenous people of the region worked for a thousand years to genetically modify their corn, selectively breeding the plant for greater size every year. It was a multicoloured 'superfood' (what humans once knew simply as 'food', not an overpriced luxury item) and came in a variety of forms for different purposes. It is still a staple in Indigenous Mesoamerica, and is very different from the sweet, yellow, generic corn most people know, which is the result of a few centuries of additional modification by Europeans to standardise it for planetary-scale production.

The Olmecs could now store dry corn to eat all year round, when they would otherwise need to move camp to a different part of their territory to access seasonally available foods. They could make permanent settlements and concentrate energy and resources to build cities. Most preferred to continue in the old ways, but some of them settled and became the Toltecs. Quetzalcoatl's appearance came from the spirit of the land (or self-organising informatics of complex ecosystems, if you prefer) to ensure that this new civilisation would be designed with reverence and care for nature, while generating great works of art, literature, science, mathematics, philosophy and engineering. He was an inspirational entity of balance between city, spirit and nature. He was a being of the wind, but also the other sacred elements of earth, water and fire, because those are the things that shape and move the wind. Eduardo tells us that this is why the number four was the foundation of his mathematical code.

The Toltecs remained mindful of his Law through constant ritual in all mundane life tasks, honoured this four-part pattern by greeting the four corners of the universe when waking to the sun, eating, washing clothes—everything. A person could never be bored or inept when every task was sacred and aligned with the spirit of a powerful Serpent. Importantly, the corn had to be sanctified in this pattern, planted in cyclic four-part algorithms that made the long hours of labour into an intellectual and spiritual process of ecstatic connection with the land. This intense connection allowed the city-builders to retain Indigenous skills and knowledge of anticipating weather, in relation with Quetzalcoatl as the bringer of rain, to optimise the timing of sowing and harvest for greater abundance. All efforts were directed towards care and reverence for land, with every activity striving to elevate and connect the material world, the surface of the earth, with the essence of spirit. This maintained the flow of nourishing energy across living systems, with humans as the conduit through Ceremony. This custodial role shaped the unique culture and style of artistic expression and urban design.

Quetzalcoatl and his people were not equipped, however, to deal with the problem of scale. There are aggregated efficiencies in upsized systems that produce greater outputs with fewer inputs of time and energy, creating a stable and regenerative order; but there are limits to scale beyond which all networks become dysfunctional, and every growth-based apparatus fails. Toltec cities like Teotihuacan became far too populous to maintain when the arrow of urban growth overtook the arrow of Ceremonial increase. There is only so much ritual convergence possible on the plane of a city grid aligned ritually with the four corners of the universe. It's simple maths, which we're sure Quetzalcoatl had his people working with in the beginning, but at some stage they must have forgotten to do their homework.

Was their civilisational collapse a result of the age-old complaint that 'Lazy kids these days don't know how good they've got it'? Were some Gen Z Toltec kids sitting in class saying, 'Ω is Teotihuacan's domain of the plane with a boundary marked by four points a, b, c, d, and if we apply a critical site-percolation model on the intersection of Ω with δT for every $\delta > 0$, um, then, a cluster connecting the arcs ab and cd…Aah, fuck this! Let's go play patolli!'

Maybe it was the inevitable decline that comes with hierarchies, when the domination of a priestly class sucks the agency and resources out of the middle and lower classes. In that scenario, knowledge always becomes capital, which must be encrypted as complicated bullshit to prevent access and social mobility. Maybe that societal pyramid is the centre of the death vortex of civilisations. The Toltecs certainly built a few stone monstrosities shaped that way. In the early days, rocks were considered sentient beings and brethren, but eventually they became just another resource, and sustainable cities of soil became tombs of stone.

Perhaps the poor bastards hauling bricks lost the will to bless the four directions with every heave of quarried basalt and every breath of choking lime dust, and the slaves flogged bloody in the fields lost the rhythm of Quetzalcoatl's quadratic formula. Maybe the game theory nerds are right, and once the population grew large enough for anonymity and personal privacy, the grifters and freeloaders spawned enough welfare queens to destroy the civilisation. Eduardo simply says, 'When you put together so many people, something failing, I think, my friends.'

Whatever your preferred theory may be, the result was still the same: Quetzalcoatl left the building. Some stories hold that he died, and Eduardo will only admit that he 'went away'. We have met people who say that he migrated to a land of red and black, and we have asked many of our own Elders if a winged Serpent arrived here in our land of red soil and black soil in the last millennium, but nobody has claimed him yet. The Toltec followed the usual sequence of civilisations—a thousand years of genetic modification of crops, a thousand years of expansion, and a thousand years of decline and devastation. Somewhere in the final phase, their Serpent spirit departed in despair. We wonder how much longer our own Rainbow Snake will tolerate this mess, and where he will go if he leaves us.

It would be so easy to blame the decline of the Toltecs on the Spanish invasion, but Quetzalcoatl left centuries before that occurred, and the civilisation was in the final stages of its demise when the conquistadors arrived. If anything, the invasion was a wake-up call. Ninety percent of their population was wiped out in four years, and the survivors spent the next five hundred years recovering their spiritual connection with the land and keeping the spirit of their feathered Serpent alive through daily ritual and cycles of Ceremony. Each generation has become stronger, and now they carry more than just the wisdom of nature—they also preserve compelling cautionary tales about the catastrophes that occur when communities abandon that wisdom, as well as upholding a successful use-case for recovery after such disasters.

The key to the Mesoamerican renaissance model is reconnection with Serpent spirit. The good thing about snake-like creator beings is that their death or departure does not take them to a different plane beyond existence, like heaven or hell. Instead, they are integrated into our world through the non-binary reality of unified opposites. In Quetzalcoatl's case, the cycles of light and darkness create a metaphysical loophole for continuity beyond his demise, if people continue to work with the old Law in their ceremonial role as a custodial species.

Eduardo explains this to us in ways we are familiar with from Sunrise-Sunset Dreaming. Venus is a planet that can announce the dusk or herald the dawn, and it has a dark side where Quetzalcoatl's twin brother lives. The land of red and black is the dark side of worlds as they turn, and the darkness is needed because if everything is white and eternally bright, then all things must die. The cycle of death and loss is what brings life and regeneration, and if that turnaround is enacted in Ceremony and ritualised in people's daily tasks, then the Serpent abides in the living world.

Theocratic hierarchies, on the other hand, reflect a binary cosmology in which spirit is separated from reality and is housed in an otherworld of heaven or hell, dooming us to live in a universe of dominion, struggle and eternal consequence. Reunification of land, people and spirit in these necrotic systems can only occur through apocalypse, the death of the world, to realign existence with the dead kingdom of the dead god (and thus restoring the deceased to life). Snakes can be nasty, it's true, but not that bloody nasty. Climate change and global warfare are probably not part of Quetzalcoatl's plans for creation.

Eduardo describes for us the way celestial cycles and Mesoamerican calendars have always aligned like clockwork with seasons and Ceremony, until last century when the climate began to shift in ways that could no longer be reconciled with the stars. His people, however, had reason to rejoice when they saw a temporary realignment of the old calendars and rainfall during the lockdowns of the global COVID-19 pandemic. Some in his community say that this happened because planes were not flying around and disturbing Quetzalcoatl in the clouds.

Oh! So perhaps Serpent spirit is not dead or lost in this world. Maybe there is spirit still in the land, and it hasn't all been sucked away to some gated community of ascended patriarchs in another dimension. What if the Jehovah's Witnesses are right, and there are no more vacancies left in heaven, so our eternal reward following a global reset will be to live in an earthly paradise of natural bounty? It's good to sit and have a cup of tea with them rather than yelling at them when they come knocking, because paradise on earth with caring community is a sweet way of picturing the end of the world. But where does Quetzalcoatl belong in this cosmic landscaping project?

Eduardo laughs on our computer screen and notes that it is evening here for us, but daytime where he is, so we are currently on the dark side. And yet we still exist! Therefore, object permanence can survive the limits of scale, and that liminal moment between the opening and closing of your eyes is where Quetzalcoatl abides. Oh my goodness, does this mean we have proven that Serpent spirit is real by referencing legitimate academic theory within a metaphysical analogy?

No, Eduardo was laughing because knowledge doesn't work like that. That's a trick used by woo-woo thought leaders to make their silly claims seem plausible and get you to credit their illusions without question. There is danger in directly applying mythical reasoning to all kin-making, meaning-making, sense-making and change-making in our lived reality, and it is important to remember that extended metaphors are abstractions, not literal instructions for acting upon the world. They are useful for bridging the divide between intuitive genius and rigorous inquiry, providing sacred protocols of care and mindful relationships with the land and each other in our lives and work. But truth claims take a bit more time and humility, so don't get too carried away with our stories here.

In other words, the universe is not a cosmic shopping platform where you can purchase privilege with positive thoughts, deep breathing and half-arsed references to quantum physics. If we were to tell you about morpho-resonant didgeridoo frequencies while painting your face for a kangaroo yoga workshop and recommending bush medicine supplements, please tell us you wouldn't fall for that shit. We have seen supposedly Olmec and Toltec self-help books that follow that pattern of new-age bastardy, and we even have one of them on our bookshelf. But these pseudo-spiritual fantasies bear very little resemblance to the living culture and spirit of the Quetzalcoatl Lore that Eduardo has shared with us.

Humans from antiquity have always honoured the wisdom of intuition and lived experience to help make sense of the world, but we have always had Lore to measure against our findings, and Law to align us in right relation. Our relations have always formed pools of intuition and experience shared in a constant process of peer review towards consensus. In our present reality relations are fractured, Lore is only half-remembered, and Law is obscured with reactive laws and individual opinions. People still operate from their lived experience, but as individuals or interest groups, and their intuition is a customised experience that feels like empowerment but is actually making them vulnerable to manipulation by spiritual and political powerbrokers. Science is a discipline that still employs collective experience and consensus, but people mistrust it because of 'gut feelings' and isolated experiences that have been skewed in their perception by master manipulators with agendas beyond their understanding. There are some spiritual traditions and religious sects that avoid this exploitation, but many lean into it with vicious enthusiasm, playing on uncertainty and fear of individual mortality.

Us-two are not completely in agreement about all of this. One of us knows that there is a creator in another world who can be reached with prayer and may help us when we ask, and one of us doesn't know that. We both know there are creation entities and ancestors in the land that we must call out to for permission and safety when we access different places, but we can't hassle them with our personal thoughts, hopes and fears in prayerful communion. We agree that there's no point praying to the Serpent, and it is probably a good idea not to mess with his raw Law by disturbing him with praises and requests. A creation entity that might kill you if you open your eyes underwater or approach the ocean's edge with fish fat on your mouth is probably not someone you want to bother about curing your cataracts or getting a new car. All we can do is flow with the Law in the land and avoid transgressions.

Eduardo's Quetzalcoatl is far more approachable and amenable to constant spiritual contact. His people connect with him in mundane rituals constantly, which gives them a kind of grounded spirituality that keeps them anchored to the miracle of life in this world. In this way they have recovered from their previous experiments with the self-terminating systems of civilisation-building, redesigning an Indigenous way of being that is sustainable in modernity. It demands discipline to be in good relation with this earth, to worry less about other worlds you might access by levelling up through magical alliances with ghostly monarchs. Serpent spirit is supposed to give us a sense of eternity that is both comforting and unsettling, to anchor us in this reality rather than conjuring illusions of an ever-after.

The hope of immortality is a hell of a drug.

SNAKES ON AN INFINITE PLANE

We're staying by a lake on Lenape land in upstate New York and the land is silent. Nothing has moved or made a sound since we arrived the night before, because we are strangers in this place and the people of the land have not greeted us or brought us in the right way. It is a corporate retreat. Four of us are Aboriginal and there are some black and brown people with us, but there are a lot of cowboys and no Indians at this lake, unless you count our friend Parul Punjabi Jagdish, who is from India (where European explorers thought they had landed when they first set foot on Turtle Island—hence the confusing label given to Native

Americans). English is becoming an awkward tongue to use in multicultural modernity, when all the people and places and things in the world were named by bad navigators with ophidiophobia (fear of snakes). But Parul is talking to us about thanatophobia (fear of death), while the living forest around the lake is silent as the grave.

Parul lives a life of free-range kin-making, a one-man embassy who travels the world in service, speaking many languages and testing the limits of how many strong relationships one human can hold. His parents were from Pakistan and Indigenous groups in central India, but he grew up in southern India in a forested valley by a sacred mountain, around a family altar populated by Sikh, Hindu and Buddhist gods, along with a few Serpents as well.

He has a snake ring on his finger from his home village. It is a symbol of Shiva, the god of destruction, a being so old that he predates the ancient Ayurvedic tradition. He is old enough to be a contemporary of primal Nagas and Naginis (male and female Serpents). As such, he is a keeper of knowledge about destruction and death as transformation, the shedding of skin, the cycles of birth and rebirth, the venom that is both poison and medicine.

In our yarns together, we weave in our stories of the Rainbow Serpent and bodies of water, including cautionary tales about approaching lakes without observing the proper protocols of respect and introduction. We decide to do our entrance rituals at the water's edge, calling out for the old people there to hear our languages, our names and our purpose, physically interacting with the earth and water to make the spirits of the place familiar with our scent.

Soon there is a puff of wind ruffling the mirror surface of the lake and a bullfrog begins to call out in a voice so loud that it sounds like it is coming from a creature as big as a horse. A squirrel darts between the trees, then another. A fish bursts from the surface, then six more in quick succession. A family of geese on the far shore emerges from reeds and now there are squirrels everywhere. Eagle calls from overhead. Chickadees flitter around the bushes and a woodpecker starts his tapping.

We understand that perception comes with filters. The argument could be made that these things were already going on by the lake and we just didn't notice until we did the ritual. But in our culture, we would say, 'Country is opening up for us.' This means that, if we continue with respect, the land will share things with us and we will share in return. We all agree that this is what has occurred, then make jokes about wishing the forest would provide us with some meat, because Parul's vegetarian friends have organised the catering, and there's only so much rice and legumes an Aboriginal person can eat!

A deer flashes past in the forest. Two snakes slither out of the reeds and stretch out in the warm sun, one green and one black, and the Aboriginal men present sit a while and ponder this as the snakes move off and draw attention to the game trails in the forest. Along those trails, a second small deer is spotted, and it doesn't run off like the other one did. There are no spears with us, but there are plenty of rocks, and soon we have our meat.

Whatever team-building exercises, training and meetings are planned for that day are soon forgotten in the excitement of butchering the deer and the rituals of preparing a feast. The sudden violence, the shocking death, the stunning beauty of the herbivore's insides glowing with rainbow highlights in the sun, the awed witness as that rainbow slowly fades and the spirit moves on—these passing sights shift us all into an altered state that compels us towards ritual. But how can people express this meaning-making impulse around life and death when they are in a place where they don't belong?

How can we engage with spiritual practice in diaspora without imposing alien religiosity, or appropriating local traditions, or being performative, or suppressing that self-conscious feeling we all get when we intuit that we're being swept up in some weird bullshit? Above all, how do we include everybody present, excluding nobody, diminishing nobody, elevating nobody? How do we keep everyone's cultural integrity safe, when we are in the vulnerable altered state of ritual, and open to the persuasion of cultists, plastic shamans and cosplay gurus?

Parul is annoyed, in his gentle and loving way, when we use the word 'guru' like that, even if we specify that we are referring to the 'small g secular guru'; he would prefer that we don't profane that sacred term at all. He reminds us that Gurus are not mythological, but part of a living tradition, allowing us to come into the presence of a sacred being that is not in story, but right in front of us, 'eating soup and watching TV'. They do not seek power or proclaim themselves as Gurus. Parul warns us, 'If somebody calls themselves a Guru, run away!' Real Gurus turn the mundane into the sacred, because they are people who have awakened to their true identity as an intertwined web of relations, free from illusions of competition, hierarchy and fear of death. Parul says they are the same as very senior Elders in Australia—when people come into their presence, they feel infinite connection and peace, the dispelling of illusions and rivalry. 'Your mind clears. The deer and the lion drinking from the same trough in the presence of Buddha—it's like that.'

This brings us back to the reality of the forest by the lake on Lenape land, where a deer has been killed. This is not an unusual event in a place where people with guns like to stalk prey for sport and the land frequently falls silent and hides its secrets when strangers pass through. But today the land opened up for us as respectful relatives and gave us meat, which demands some reciprocity of spirit, energy and matter. In the absence of local traditional protocols, this ritual problem can be resolved authentically if those present are moving with Serpent spirit to understand the nature of death as a regenerative disturbance.

SNAKE TALK

Where death intersects with civilisation it can become final and destructive, a termination point imposed by stories of struggle against nature as an enemy that is red in tooth and claw. That is a bad death. Here, it must be mediated by ritual to unify creation and destruction, because, as Parul says, 'Snake is good death.' All we need to ask is how to transform every part of this carcass into a catalyst for regenerative increase in the land. If we can do that together without leaders, coaches or facilitators emerging, then our ritual will be the real deal.

'When we are in nature, death shows its face more. Leaves falling. All around, dying inside us too, cells in a dance of death and regeneration.' Parul describes it well, that snake-eyed view of mortality that moves us in ritual together. The walls and illusions of the city are gone, and this is no longer a corporate retreat, but a moment of homecoming. Importantly, everybody's belief is honoured, no matter how contradictory, and we share freely without trying to persuade or convert others.

It would be so easy to radicalise several vegans into some perverted cult of ketogenic Indigeneity right now! They've never seen guts before, or the miracle of sparkling life sinking crimson into the earth. They marvel at the elasticity of the fresh, dappled hide and the twitching of exposed muscle, the rich, yellow abundance of fat and gleaming ivory of resilient bone, some of which will probably still be around when our own bones return to the soil.

It is a revelation to observe the different parts of spirit discernible only in their departure—the conscious spirit leaving the eyes, the living spirit leaving the flesh, the ancestral spirit returning to the bloody earth and the big spirit rising to the sky, which is felt in the activities that follow. It would be unthinkable to leverage these sacred moments for coercive brain-hacking and high-pressure persuasion. As we move through this ritual, it should enfold the stories of the plant-eating people and enhance them. It's more than tolerance or inclusion—we need their stories as we work with the body of this herbivore and the plants, trees, rocks and waters all around. Their perspective will show us things we might otherwise miss.

Nobody is assigning tasks or directing the work. We are all considering what should be done and sharing our knowledge and observations. Some are discerning the flows of underground water and the patterns of game trails and scat, while others determine what parts of the carcass they want to use or return carefully to the forest. Meat and organs are distributed to people with different dishes they want to make, and the unused parts are placed with an awareness of ant, crow and water flow in a growing, collective ecological mapping of the forest system around the lake.

There are long rituals of loving care as groups form around different food preparation tasks, interspersed with periods of rest, dance, visual art, storytelling, singing and play. For some it is the right moment to move through trauma or discard damaging illusions, and there are others there who see this and sit with them in support. We are not team building here, but kin-making. Later we feast and sit around the fire deep into the night, beginning deep dialogue with Parul about Serpent spirit that will continue long after we have left the forest and the lake behind, when that campfire is only ash and memory. The next day we must return to New York City, where the collective wisdom held by land and kin in this place will dissipate amidst the demands of empire and economic need.

'Naga Naga!' Parul exclaims softly, in his customary way of invoking the sacred Serpent in mundane moments. He sees the impermanence of the retreat as a good thing. You can't become a Swami or a Guru by staying in a cave and growing your beard out—you need to make the entire world your family and live among it rather than in blissful retreats and contemplative isolation. But how can we retain the wisdom of life and death amidst the speed and pressure of psychotic cityscapes?

Parul spent his childhood in a forest valley, in a small village by a sacred mountain. He watched the village grow into a city as the forest was eradicated, and when he was ten his father passed away. He realised then that everything is impermanent. He had heard this truth and repeated it before, but it is one thing to say it and another to experience it. He later retreated from the city and spent years living with Swamis in the Himalayan wilderness, where he began to see his own mortality as a snakeskin that slides off seasonally.

'The relational thread between us is more real than this being that I perceive myself to be. Looking at death is the best way to work through anxiety, depression, trauma. We're constantly dying. If something is troubling you, it's not as big as the fact that you are going to die! It gives us the freedom to move.' When he thinks of the city that has displaced the forest village of his youth, he sees the customs and stories that remain in his neighbourhood and contemplates the ancient ruins all over India of cities from another age. The stones are weathered and swarming with vines and monkeys, and this reminder of impermanence helps him when he must spend extended periods living in the city.

He carries his traditions and practice with him in his heart, and that is how he stays grounded in metropolitan environments. The energetic economies of city life make it hard to maintain this over long periods, though. In the land, the more you put out the more you get back, but Parul observes that this doesn't work in the city. The more you give, the more you are drained. We reflect on how difficult it becomes to walk past homeless people without helping them all. How do you keep your humanity alive in that moment?

Parul says the challenge and discomfort of such moments is a gift. A person's inner compass can be found while sitting in nature, but it also needs to be tested. The pressures of the city suppress it and conflict us with painful feelings, but we have to sit with these, in our authentic selves and not the illusion. Reality is uncertainty, and pain is a signal for us to find meaning in the raw truth of this existence. Serpent stories from the southern hemisphere give us paths for achieving this wisdom—they don't have simple character arcs or clear morals, and they are complex and multi-layered, stories within stories. There is no transcendent message, or 'aha' moment. But if you sit with the stories for long enough, something opens up for you and you find meaning. The meaning is not made in peace and quiet, but in what Parul refers to as 'the churn'.

His sacred mountain is the centre of a creation story of the universe. It rests upon the back of a turtle, and there are sublime Devas and demonic Asuras struggling and churning within the mountain. The Serpent is the binding thread within the churn, tying opposing forces together as the universe is made from this titanic struggle. Shiva drinks the venom of the Naga and his throat turns blue, while the goddess of wealth appears with the elixir of immortality, coveted by Devas and Asuras alike. The trickster Vishnu transforms himself into the form of a beautiful woman and takes the elixir for the Devas so that evil cannot be nurtured in humans by demonic entities. A wily devil manages to steal some of it, but in the moment he drinks it a Deva cuts off his head. He is doomed to immortality but with a separate head and body, which float in space for all eternity as stars that keep the Lore in the night sky.

Where is the wisdom here to help us retain connection

amidst the madness of the city? Parul says it is just like our Aboriginal Lore—the answer isn't in the story itself, but in the many interconnected stories and collective lived experiences that form our narrative landscapes of meaning. He brings a small story alongside the epic of the mountain at the centre of creation, the story of a baby in the womb. The baby says, 'This time around, I will remember eternity!' But, faced with the trauma and gore of birth, the infant cries and all truth is forgotten. The little one's true self becomes hidden beneath the suffering of the world, until he can become enlightened and find it again. Within the context of the fabulous tales of demons, Nagas and Devas, this simple story leads us to understand that there is a way out of suffering, a return to your true self-in-relation, and that is the path of your life.

Your connected self is not at the end of the path, though—it is not a reward to claim at the climax of some hero's journey. Rather, it is always present, like the sun on a cloudy day. Just because you are cold and in darkness, it doesn't mean the sun is not still there. 'Clouds of anxiety and depression can cover your essential nature, the peace within. It is revealed the more you sit with yourself, not just in meditation but when doing things like chopping vegetables.'

We reflect together on the paradox of this story—that it is about object permanence (the realisation in early childhood that when you close your eyes the things in front of you still exist) within a thought-tradition that is based on the principle of impermanence. It is only a linguistic paradox, though, because in English those two concepts both happen to contain the word 'permanence', but in Sanskrit the words are different. Seeking universal meaning by reading the tea leaves of Anglo etymology seldom results in sound logic, especially when you're talking to Indians. Still, we have fun playing with English for a while, inventing new terms like 'subject permanence' and 'object impermanence' and imagine what these silly ideas might look like through the eye of the Naga, amidst the thread and the churn of creation.

'Everything disappears in the end. Even the sun will eventually burn out. Is death a magic trick? Isn't sleep a little death? As you are waking, the world rushes back in but in that moment, you are not a separate being. The longer you can stay in that the more you can remember. The less you think of yourself, that is a sign of wisdom rising.'

This is good story. It allows us to sit still amidst the panic of a world on fire and share our Lore together without terror overtaking our minds. Anxiety about mortality is what drives us to accumulate more than we need; perhaps this is why the goddess of wealth is the one who produces the elixir of immortality. Nobody will share story with you if you're sitting down scared and wanting to gobble up knowledge to enrich yourself or feel better about dying.

So, with our personal fear of death soothed for a moment, we can now look to the pathologies of the many and the question of why humans fear gods even more than their own demise. Is fear of God the key to our salvation or the cause of our destruction? Perhaps when the churn and struggle of creation is overtaken by secular wars between capital and commune, then the incentive to maintain care of all life is lost. Can there still be effective rule of law without sacred Law?

We will follow these lines of inquiry and story along the paths of many Asian Serpents, now that Parul has sung out for us and given us the name we can invoke in those lands.

Naga Naga!

AWE AND LAW IN THE HOME OF THE SNAKE

Our Naga pass from Parul takes us to Kathmandu now, where the Naag is waiting for us, along with the goddess of wealth and the burdens of drought and debt. Although us-two have only visited there 0.5 times, there have been Nepali stories in our household for the last ten years—long enough for one of us to offer a heartfelt *namaste* to our new friend Anil Chitrakar without sounding like a yoga-Karen. We share with him our story of meeting and falling in love at a campfire, and the months of separation and longing that followed when we went back to our families at opposite ends of the continent. The thing that held us in connection was

Nepali jewellery—we wore twin onyx bracelets from there to remember each other from day to day, and when we had our first child we called her Onyx.

Another household story we share with Anil is the inspiration we gained from a Nepali Indigenous radio station, dedicated to preserving traditional languages that have become endangered since Nepal 'opened up' to the modern world in the 1950s. In the twentieth century the totalising nationalisms of capitalism, communism and fascism competing for space there decimated cultural diversity, disrupting many ancient traditions. But the old ways of Kathmandu are resilient, and Anil has taken mass media to the next level since the COVID-19 pandemic, creating a new wave of online content to preserve traditional culture, economics and governance. He is also a wood carver from a family that keeps the foundational Lore of Nepali cosmology—the Serpent.

From our perspective as Aboriginal people from wood-working kin-groups, Anil's family business of wood carving is a clan specialisation in a network of sixty-four kinship groupings, all with different but interwoven skills and traditional practice. Anil describes these as syndicated guilds, and asserts, 'Don't ever use the word caste! This is not an Indian system.' It's complicated. There have been so many waves of invasion, migration and settlement there, with the rise and fall of different ethnic and religious regimes, that Kathmandu has become an incredible fusion of Indigenous, Buddhist and Hindu systems sprinkled with competing versions of capitalism and communism. China, India, Russia, Tibet, Korea and dozens more all have ideological footholds in Nepal. But for every attempt to impose caste privilege and exclusion, there are a thousand cultural caveats, alternatives and loopholes in the life of the streets, and the buck stops with the Serpent, the bringer of rain.

The common snake (which we distinguish with a lower-case 's') is seasonally prolific throughout Kathmandu. Its eradication in ancient times brought drought and death when the valley was drained to make room for human habitation, so the people learned that this reptile must be respected as the ultimate authority over continued human existence. The civilisation that followed this early occupation survived by engineering systems of coexistence with snakes, weaving together nature, infrastructure, economy, technology and (most importantly) Ceremony to create some of the most resilient urban communities on earth.

Anil tells us that the snake becomes the Naag, a 'spirited Snake', when it gains a realisation of right and wrong—not just in itself, but in the people who coexist with it. As in Aboriginal Australia, everyone knows you're never more than a few steps away from this sentient, venomous reptile in snake season, and if you do wrong by him, you're gonna get bit! The local cultures, economies and governance of street life in Kathmandu are grounded in Indigenous knowledge of the Naag. The first principle of this knowledge system is

AWE AND LAW IN THE HOME OF THE SNAKE

awareness of the fact that humans are occupying the home of the snakes, who have become Naags in order to maintain ecological balance for all and maintain the flow of water and life.

The syndicated system of guilds, which distributes Naag knowledge throughout the ritual life of the community, is the centre of production, trade and labour. There are two workplaces—the home as a location for cottage industry and the communal guild spaces for intensive production. Artisans like Anil move between these for different projects. He says this traditional system is very resilient; for example, there was minimal disruption to the local economy during COVID-19 lockdowns, because working from home was already the norm in Kathmandu. The resilience of the workforce is mostly due to the interdependent guild network that governs the means of production, which is embedded in the living spaces and street life of the workers. In this relational economy, the woodblock sculptures that Anil's guild creates for the endless rounds of festivals and Ceremony in the Nepali calendar are used as casts by other guilds (don't say caste!) to create reliefs in the materials each group specialises in—gold, copper, stone, brick, ceramics and so forth. They are also used for printmaking on paper and fabric, and as models for motifs in jewellery.

Various pieces from different guilds are assembled as altars, adornments and installations for temples, homes, communal spaces and public buildings. Every work of art produced for local ritual use and the massive international export market is a collective effort—Anil says no masterpiece in his culture is ascribed to an individual genius but is credited to multiple guilds and craftspeople. Profits are circulated throughout this cooperative system, and nothing goes to waste. When everyone is finished using the woodblocks from Anil's guild, they are expertly painted to become sacred objects in their own right (and products for sale in a high-demand marketplace). In the Nepali way, it is not the object that has value—the syndicated relationships that produce the object, and the extended kinship embedded in sacred nature, are the things that represent economic value. Further, with no single creator being rewarded with wealth and celebrity status, there are no limitations of copyright or intellectual property, so the creative commons gives rise to an incredible proliferation of unique art that is coveted by collectors worldwide.

We ask Anil what prevents the 'tragedy of the commons' in this system—how do Nepalese avoid the emergence of bad actors leveraging copyright law to corner markets, undercut competitors, install monopolies and enslave workers? There have certainly been historical attempts by powerbrokers to install class systems of enslavable and non-enslavable castes, with mixed results. How do Nepalese communities prevent the lawlessness that inevitably arises when people undermine the commons in pursuit of personal wealth and power?

In most monotheistic cultures, wealth is concentrated

and held by elites, and this property is protected by the fear of God and violence against the declared enemies of God. Admittedly, this also happens in polytheistic cultures, as can be seen in the religious innovations of Hindu fascism, where the God of creation is placed above all and represented by an elite Brahman caste. This is not necessarily the case in Nepal, where the formless Brahma is found in nature rather than temples. The powerful Naag is placed at the base of most religious shrines and buildings, where the ground beneath an idol's feet is more important than the crown on his head. So, if a universal fear of God is not used to incentivise adherence to the rule of law in Nepal, then what is holding their sacred commons together?

Anil's answer is expansive and illuminating, but it is not simple. We will try to do it justice here as we summarise his complex weaving of stories within stories and lessons within lessons. He begins by telling us that while there are no temples or images in his community for Brahma, the creator, there are many for Shiva, the destroyer, and Vishnu, the maintainer. He describes the physics of this as positive, negative and neutral forces in constant tension and balance, mediated by the ritual observances of the people in symbiotic relation with nature. The Buddha is also present in his many forms, as a deity of impermanence and change.

Shiva is represented in human form and honoured as a force of entropy and renewal, while Vishnu's image is revered in ritual governance of household and guild economies, as well as communal care for infrastructure embedded in natural systems. Administration is also his domain, although the people don't concern themselves much with this, leaving politicians to worry about things like the alarming escalation of national debt (which is almost half of Nepal's GDP). Shiva is celebrated in moments of cataclysm like earthquakes and floods because these require massive rebuilding and redecorating efforts, stimulating local production and periodically boosting the economy and industry of street life.

We were interested to hear that Anil's people hold crows sacred because in times of impending disaster they all call out frantically as a warning, just as they did in the 2015 earthquakes, giving most residents time to evacuate their homes. Every apocalyptic event in Nepal is perceived as a divine act of regeneration for humans in concert with nature. Floods are seen as cleansing and fertilising the land—all crises represent a chance for a new beginning, like the informal debt jubilees the community organises periodically to allow everyone a fresh start.

Debt forgiveness is a sacred obligation, and when it is done on a momentous scale it is always marked historically as the beginning of a new era. Anil jokes that if Microsoft were to pay off the national debt of Nepal, then they would move into year one of the Bill Gates era. In that event, Bill might end up with shrines and temples and statues dedicated to his image, just like Shiva and Vishnu. However, Brahma does not have these things because he is all of creation, so he is represented by wild entities like animals and plants rather than as a human figure. This promotes an ethos that is not exactly a fear of God, but an all-consuming awe of land and nature, alongside joyful acceptance of acts of God such as natural disasters, epidemics or financial crises—these are not punitive moments of divine retribution, but gifts of renewal and abundance. The righteous vengeance of God is not a thing to fear in Nepal.

But without sacred Law to regulate human activity, there can be no water, and without that most sacred substance there is only death. The Nepalese awe of nature is most strikingly embodied in the symbiotic holy trinity of frog, snake and mongoose that their water infrastructure is built upon. This is not based on superstition, but a truly miraculous biological partnership and a vast, ingenious feat of engineering.

Stories within stories! Tragedy of the commons, carved deities, disasters, debt and now another subplot! These threads will resolve as we sit quietly and listen, remembering that the 'figure and ground' cognitive orientation of non-western cultures is reversed, and context is all. This storyscape will yet reveal the secrets of maintaining rule of law in the commons.

Anil begins the snake-frog-mongoose trinity story by observing that in Europe the high ground in cities is reserved for the palaces and castles of the mighty, but in Nepal the highest ground of every town or city is for forestry and watersheds. A hundred days of rain per year falls upon the trees and is held beneath the roots for the long dry season that follows. It is filtered as it flows through wetland ponds and trickles underground to emerge in springs that feed into canals and rice paddies, resources held in trust as a commons for the community to use and care for together. From there it goes underground to the urban areas, flowing through an elaborate system of ancient ceramic pipes no thicker than an adult's thigh, emerging at frequent points throughout the city in beautifully carved waterspouts where people collect the water, before it flows on to the river below.

This network of fragile cylinders beneath the earth should not work, because they ought to become clogged with obstructions and muck within a couple of seasons, halting the flow of clean water, and they cannot be cleared by hand as they are inaccessible. But this is where the magic of the symbiotic trinity comes in. When the Ceremony that summons the snakes (and therefore the wet season) is completed, the frogs arrive and lay their eggs in the water. The tadpoles wriggle through the half-clogged pipes and quickly grow into adulthood, feasting on all the bugs that have infested the system, and the snakes enter to hunt the fat frogs. This loosens a lot of the blockages, but the pipes are still dirty. If only there were something furry that we could run through them like a pipe cleaner or a bottle brush... Oh! Here comes the mongoose, chasing the snakes! This seasonal symbiosis is what has kept the plumbing of the city maintained for millennia.

As Aboriginal people, we share Anil's view of this sacred set of relations as more than a series of encounters between predators and prey in a violent food chain. Our biological science is not influenced by Rudyard Kipling stories of heroic mongooses battling evil cobras to protect British children in India. There are no zero-sum games of contest between rivalrous species in our culture or Anil's. We are embedded in conscious systems of land where every kill involves many sentient beings and distributes benefit regeneratively to create abundance. Our ecologies are collaborative communities where predator and prey may drink from the same waterhole and even provide assistance to each other when needed. In floods, for example, you may catch a glimpse of small animals catching a ride on the back of a swimming snake. When we understand biology like this we can create abundant ways of life, whether we are hunter-gatherers or city-dwellers. It only works, though, when we have Ceremony designed to hold us in awe of natural entities.

In Kathmandu this awe is maintained daily with ritual observances that change with the seasons and major Ceremonies that proliferate throughout their lunar calendar, which coexists in contradictory but happy relation with the solar Gregorian calendar. Just as most ritual objects and shrines have Snakes at their base, Anil says that every prayer, event, festival and Ceremony begins with a call-out to the

Naags—'Snakes! Forgive us for occupying your place!' Effectively, land acknowledgement protocols in Kathmandu uniquely recognise non-humans as First Peoples.

The driest season is in the month of April, and in the Nepali worldview drought equals suffering, which is the opposite of their concept of compassion. So, at that time, they hold Karunāmaya, the Festival of the Chariot, dedicated to The Compassionate One. It lasts almost a month, until the first rains arrive and deliver compassion from the sky. The huge chariot is made up of many wooden pieces that are carved by Anil's guild, according to numbers and measurements representing sacred tenets of the Buddhist faith. The massive structure is assembled following ancient design principles that provide the people with a blueprint for building earthquake-resistant houses. The most important piece of the chariot is the central beam underneath, which is carved to signify the Naag. The procession of the chariot represents pulling the snake into the valley, as the seasonal appearance of snakes in great numbers heralds the coming of the monsoon.

There is a moment in the festival where a human girl who is proclaimed a living goddess is paraded before the people, a ritual act that Anil offers as an example of sacred Law enforcing secular law through god-fearing principles. It is another narrative digression in his web of stories within stories, but we feel the big-picture context emerging in such details. 'The relevance is, you know, the way to protect a young girl in our society is not by laws or by police, but by declaring them divine.' However, this is a 'fear of god' disincentive, which is quite different from the awe of nature inspired by the Naags. With one in five Nepali women reporting experiences of intimate partner violence, and around half of Nepali men agreeing that domestic violence is justified if a woman leaves the house without permission, it seems that divinity doesn't provide much of a shield against abuse.

Around the world there is often a mythical connection between Serpents and women, but this relationship in Indigenous traditions is weakened by our induction into new traditions that settle our hearts and cast out our paragons of creation and fertility. These new traditions sing hard words into our troubled minds. 'Cursed are you above all livestock and all wild animals! You will crawl on your belly and you will eat dust all the days of your life. And I will put enmity between you and the woman, and between your offspring and hers; he will crush your head, and you will strike his heel.' But we will grapple with this later as we follow the path of the Naga across Asia. For now, we will temper our admiration of Kathmandu traditions with an awareness of the difficulties and abuses that face many Nepali women as they fall through the cracks of sacred protection and Naag Law, which are frequently disrupted by competing economies, traditions and truths. This is a good moment to remember that no single tradition contains all of the answers for saving the world, and that our reality is made up of complex and troubling layers at every turn.

Anil's weave of stories within stories continues with a description of the first rains of the monsoon season, when the people are in the fields planting seeds. The water table is still low for another month or two as gravity slowly does its work, so in June there is a day of Ceremony dedicated to cleaning the wells, which are decorated with two Serpents coiled around them, signifying that beneath the ground humans are entering the realm of the Naags. A lamp is lit and lowered into the well, where it may be extinguished by the carbon monoxide breath of a Naag if he is angry, in which case the Ceremony must be postponed, as the gas is a sign that the water flow has been delayed (and that those entering will die). If the lamp keeps burning, then the people may safely clean and repair the inside of the wells and hold a feast at the end of the day. By the lunar calendar, five days after the first full moon in July, the water table rises, and the people hold a Snakes Day festival to thank the Naags for bringing the water to the valley. Water can heal, water can destroy, and water can maintain life with compassion.

'In the Hindu pantheon, plus, minus and neutral is a cycle,' Anil says. 'And you need all three, otherwise we would not have any change, you know, which is something that we have to accept. And so, the Buddha in his deathbed, in his last sermon said, *go forth, with diligence, because everything is about to change. Nothing is going to be static.*'

AWE AND LAW IN THE HOME OF THE SNAKE

Nepal has certainly faced an influx of complex changes since it 'opened up' to the world in the 1950s. Anil's grandfather's generation sent urban planners to the United States to learn about development, and they returned with the notion that a developed nation must speak English. Education was reformed as a system of English-speaking schools, so many local dialects fell into disuse along with thousands of years of intangible heritage. In the 1970s, Tibetans fleeing Chinese occupation sought refuge in Kathmandu and brought their carpet-weaving industry with them. Soon Nepalese carpets became highly prized commodities in the international marketplace and wool was imported from New Zealand along with dyes from Switzerland. Anil describes this cultural innovation in response to marketplace demands as 'the world's biggest scam'. The industry polluted the river, and the workers began to lose their awe of sacred waters and ritual practices acknowledging the Snakes. Drought and death followed as the gravity-defying physics of extractive economies took hold of the valley.

Capital flows uphill to the elevated wealthy classes, while the toxic damage it causes flows downhill along with tainted waterways, externalities that do not appear on any balance sheet. This makes the lives of workers precarious as the cost of living escalates and income stagnates—a situation that has afflicted workers in Kathmandu and caused them to worry about the sting of unpaid bills more than the risk of snakebite. But awe of Lakshmi, the goddess of wealth, may have helped to restore good relations with the Naags in subsequent decades. When the water became polluted, people began buying clean water harvested from the high ground above the city at twenty rupees a bottle. When the value of the watershed was quantified as a commodity worth 600 million rupees per day, the secular signals of the marketplace incentivised a renewed interest in caring for waterways. When we think about it, though, in this example the incentive to care may be better attributed to fear or, rather, love of Mammon, the New Testament demon of wealth, rather than love of the goddess Lakshmi.

Anil says that wealth in the Nepali worldview means obligation, so Lakshmi's festival every November has played a pivotal role in nudging the secular incentives of capital back towards sacred Law and reverence of the Naags. Anil is yarning with us in the week before this festival, explaining the traditional economic principles that inform the Ceremony. Families begin by gathering all the precious items of value they own and decorating their homes with them, making their assets transparent to all in the community. It is essentially an annual audit for every household, whose aspiration for the new year is to begin anew without debt. Being debt-free does not begin at a balance of zero, however, as the accounting system of traditional Nepali finance must allow for late rains—for example, every home must have a seed bank exceeding what is needed for planting, in case drought falls and the first planting of crops fails. The concept of a small surplus as the starting point for calculating deficit is nested in the sacred water system, which is designed to hold an extra three or four weeks of water storage to offset the risk of late monsoons. The fraction of this annual water reserve is applied to household finance, as a ratio determining the surplus point beyond which measurement of a family's wealth begins. Wealth beyond a family's needs is regarded as what Anil translates as 'obligation', so that financially secure families may feel a spiritual duty to assist others less fortunate, or even forgive debts.

Anil asserts that this is neither capitalism nor communism, both of which have certainly taken root in Nepali politics since the 1960s through the foreign influence of the US, China, North Korea and the Soviet Union. Awe of Lakshmi and the Naags has ensured some continuity of informal economies based on traditions of maintaining the commons, despite the machinations of political parties. For many, this provides an alternative to the forced choice between political models on the modern continuum of fascism, capitalism, socialism and communism. Kathmandu is a messy site of Indigenous embassy that incorporates many cultural systems but remains grounded in traditional principles of compassion as abundance, wealth as obligation, and respect for the sacred.

Anil's complex weave of stories within stories has left us with a sense of potential solutions to global crises of meaning and money, but also a sense of uncertainty. We are now wondering about the impact of the goddess in Kathmandu's revitalisation of nature-centred street economies and governance. Is it sacred wealth or the sacred feminine that has ensured the continuity of good relations between the people and the Serpent, through an era of disruption and escalating foreign influence?

Perhaps the path of the divine feminine is the best approach to recovering ways to coexist with nature. Still, the wail of the wounded feminine troubles our sleep and makes it difficult for us to proclaim any kind of spiritual belief as a unique source of the solutions needed to save our dying world. The goddess tempts us onto another path now, as we say *namaste* to Anil Chitrakar and seek the fruits of the Naga across Asia and beyond.

EVE, THE SNAKE WOMAN

There are Nagas in Myanmar, and we are keen to meet them, but it's complicated. They were introduced by a Buddhist sect with some troubling borderwork practices involving Muslims, women, Indigenous groups and anyone else whose bad karma places them at the bottom of the nation's autocratic hierarchy. We will follow that sect to Indonesia and China, but first we must settle our confusions and contradictory stories about Woman and Serpent, as we come into relation with a land of incredible cultural diversity that is wracked with civil war and passionate resistance to absolute power and control.

SNAKE TALK

There are many different First Peoples in Myanmar, but when us-two heard about a Burmese tribe called Naga we were excited for a moment, until we discovered that this was another one of those thoughtless designations conferred by the British Empire. It was casually applied to a group of over seventy distinct nations in the north of Myanmar, probably when somebody in a safari suit visited the region after a tour in India and noticed the reverence and respect locals held for Burmese pythons.

This reverence is not undeserved. All snakes are either honoured or feared around the world, for the uncanny intersection of their longevity as a species and their miraculous capacity to mutate and evolve rapidly, but Burmese pythons are exceptional. They are almost preternaturally adaptable, which is why their DNA held the key to scientists unlocking the genomic sequence of serpentine phenotypic plasticity and metabolic adaptation. Roughly translated, that means their organs, skeletons and eyes can evolve quickly in real-time responses to changes in locality and conditions.

This makes them good pets until they become too big, a phenomenon of accelerated growth that some people ascribe to the pythons' long-term plan to eat their owners. Our Australian Aboriginal Lore about carpet pythons makes us intensely aware of the patient, strategic minds of these creatures, which are similar to their Burmese cousins. We know that they are still and slow beings, until suddenly they are not. Anyone who has seen a video of a python eating a dog or a pig knows how fast they can stretch and change their head, jaws, skin and belly to perform horrific feats of physical transformation in just a few minutes.

Nobody dreads the adaptability of the Burmese python more than the precarious underclasses of Florida, who rely on the 'opportunity' offered by the gig economy to survive from day to day as Uber drivers and snake catchers. As abandoned pets, the pythons have adapted and thrived in the Everglades, causing a sharp drop in biodiversity that has been measured by a massive decrease in the frequency of road kills in the region. (This data collection method makes good sense to us, but it also makes us feel baffled and a little sad.) The gig workers scour the wetlands for Burmese pythons to kill so they can collect a small bounty. Terrible work, if you can get it. Wrestling a five-metre snake to catch it by the head and kill it before it bites or strangles you is not the safest occupation, especially when your prey is constantly adapting to changing conditions, including the habits and techniques of its human hunters. The novel species emerging in this poorly managed landscape is always full of surprises.

Human females also undergo frequent periods of rapid biological change that have always been mysterious and terrifying for men, so it makes sense that women and snakes are often paired in a mythical association. Both are mistrusted, but are also sources of fascination and subliminal longing. In Myanmar, there is a lot of Lore involving sexualised pairings between pythons and women, including many forms of the *Beauty and the Beast* narrative. In all these stories, a low-status woman marries a python who turns into a high-status man on their wedding night, but this is not the 'happily ever after' ending that features in the European fairytale equivalent. In the second half of the tale, another woman tries the same trick, but her serpentine groom does not transform—he just eats her. There are many old stories in Myanmar of Snake-women. The Kachin tale of a man marrying a Dragon lady called Na Ga Num is still an important part of wedding ceremonies today, in which the bride wears a dress made of silver scales and must pass through kumba leaves to remove the stink of the Serpent.

Us-two have found so many stories around the world of women and snakes in various scenarios of sin and sexual tension that we're tempted to see a pattern and draw hasty conclusions from it. We're not big fans of proclaiming stories as universal human myths—this is the slack thinking that gave rise to the idea of a generalised human 'hero's journey' myth, which is inspiring for disgruntled contrarians but pretty much nobody else. In this case, however, it might be safe to say that stories of women in sexually charged relationships with magical Serpents form a common theme in traditional stories on every continent.

Have you ever been to a strip club where there is a snake act? It's usually performed by the stripper with the poorest dancing skills, who moves languidly with a python draped about her shoulders, occasionally stroking and positioning the snake in ways that suggest he might be some kind of massive sentient cock. It is a primal male fetish and, as with all such fetishes, it is projected onto women as sin. This is an old story, from an age of transition in which men and male gods carried out a coup to establish a new order of supremacy for their gender. This coup exploded across the Middle East, North Africa and the Mediterranean, and it involved slaying Serpents, subduing women and criminalising this sacred interspecies connection.

In Ancient Greek Lore, Gaea was the earth mother goddess and one of her children was a giant python who protected a holy site called Pytho, where an oracle resided. Gaea's nemesis Apollo was a bit of a 'no means yes' kind of fella who frequently punished and destroyed women when they rejected him or fled his advances. He decided, as many men do, that the fault in these violent encounters lay with the flawed females he pursued, so he decided to become a men's rights extremist, staging a series of terrorist attacks and an insurrection at Pytho to make Greece great again. He slew the python and occupied the sacred site, which he renamed Delphi as he ascended to the apex of a new hierarchical pantheon. Some say he did this because the python had sex with his mother, so perhaps the attack was not entirely unprovoked; but, whatever his motivations were, the result was the subjugation of both Serpent and woman under Bronze Age male rule.

While we have found hundreds of examples of this 'slay

the snake, subdue the woman' narrative, we need only to note the pattern and move on to expressions of the Serpent in contemporary Myanmar. We're not following the Greek stories or even the First Peoples' stories into that land, because we are still on the trail of the Naga that our friend Parul set us on. We will focus our exploration on Hindu and Buddhist traditions, including intersections with Lore from China that will lead us into encounters with imperial Dragons.

Soe Yu Nwe is the perfect guide to help us track snake-women from the mythical past to multicultural modernity. She is an artist of Chinese descent who was raised in the traditions of Myanmar, where every lake has a shrine dedicated to the Naga. She makes delicate, detailed ceramic sculptures that form narrative bridges between different eras and cultures, situated in an explosive present of brutish cruelty and terror. Her home is a hard place to be for anyone who is not a male, fascist thug. There have only ever been two free and fair elections there, both of which rejected military dictatorship and elected a democratic party led by a woman called Aung San Suu Kyi, who had previously been imprisoned for nearly fifteen years for winning a prior election that was neither free nor fair. Then, after a military coup in 2021, she was imprisoned again, where she remains.

The November 2020 election was the same year and month as the US election that ended the first Trump regime, and echoed the same conspiracy claims of rigged voting and childish tantrums over the transition of power. The

EVE, THE SNAKE WOMAN

Myanmar coup followed close on the heels of the US insurrection on 6 January 2021, as bully-boy autocrats around the world began bolstering each other's confidence to act out their fascist fantasies. Our friend Soe Yu watched military trucks from her window, which were patrolling the streets and abducting democratic party supporters. The next day, she awoke to find there was no internet or phone service, and people were panic-buying staple foods, while big companies that had been forewarned about the coup completed the evacuation of their employees to neighbouring countries. Soon, young people were being recruited into guerilla groups and moving from the city to the jungle to train as resistance fighters.

A civil war ensued that has been raging ever since, with the fascist regime terrorising the population with rape, torture, mass murder and a bombing campaign that makes Russia's assaults on Ukraine look like cheap fireworks. China is funding these military operations (along with anonymous private donors), while western nations offer minimal support to the resistance in the form of humanitarian aid. This all but dried up when funding was withdrawn by the second Trump administration. Our yarns with Soe Yu have an unreal quality, as she shows us her delicate sculpture of the Serpent Queen while women are targeted for assault and abduction to spread terror in the streets and villages all around her. As Aboriginal people, we get it, though. Life goes on, even during wars, genocides and invasions.

The ceramic figure is wearing a Naga headdress, and her liminal body is frozen in a moment of transformation as a reptilian tail emerges behind her. Soe Yu tells us about the influence of Indonesian Buddhism on Myanmar and the elaborate pagodas built by the monks, many of which are inhabited by Burmese pythons that are cared for as sacred beings. There is a pagoda in her local area, which has a small temple dedicated to the Dragon Queen at its entrance. The queen was once a human woman who lived in the early twentieth century and was deified as a protector of treasures from the underworld, or of the secret wealth that people want to conceal. Those entering the pagoda whisper their wishes to her and if the wishes come true they return with offerings to repay their debt to her. It is a popular destination for Thai pilgrims—which highlights for us the massive scope of multicultural exchange we have encountered across Asia, all with threads of connection woven together by the Serpent.

The Indonesian monks who have had such a strong influence on the faith, government and culture of Myanmar are descendants of a sect that originally migrated from China. The Naga that is carved and painted near the Buddha in most pagodas is more like a dragon than those we have seen so far, but more serpent-like than the Chinese forms. Soe Yu is also influenced by the Chinese culture of her ancestors, in particular by the story of Nuwa, a creation entity with the head of a woman and the body of a snake.

EVE, THE SNAKE WOMAN

Nuwa is celebrated in Chinese Buddhism and Confucianism, and is credited with the creation of human beings. Her medium for this was clay, as is the case in many spiritual stories around the world. Jewish theology has long held that Adam, the first man, was created from clay and that his name was derived from *adamah,* which means red clay. But Nuwa used yellow clay—for the nobility and the rich, at least. Apparently, she made commoners (or 'cord-made' people) by dragging a string through brown mud. Little wonder the Chinese-Indonesian monks of Myanmar exercise so much influence in the militarised government; the idea of a divinely mandated hierarchy is always popular with despots, who often like to apply this uneven power structure to gender. This results in unhealthy borderwork practices that seldom turn out well for women.

Soe Yu tells us that many pagodas deny entrance to females, and that most have sections where women and girls must stop at a boundary and pray at a distance from sacred objects. She gives the example of Kyaiktiyo Pagoda, which is perched atop a massive boulder teetering on the edge of a cliff. The rock is said to contain strands of Buddha's hair and is covered with gold leaf, plastered across its surface by male devotees. Women are not allowed to approach it, because legend holds that long ago it used to hover in the air until a woman touched it and diminished its power. Soe Yu says that women are considered tainted from birth, that they are seen as a negative spiritual force that drains the power of men. She was taught at school that enlightenment can only be attained if you are born into a male body. Aung San Suu Kyi may be loved and respected by the people, but she cannot rule, and her elevated status is a proxy position held in the name of her famous father, who led the fight for Burmese independence back in the day.

Many of Soe Yu's ceramic figures are beautiful women marred with physical injuries to represent both the wounded feminine and the sacred feminine. Their beauty is not erotic, as the figures exude a sense of hidden, mysterious power inspired by the transformative nature of the Serpent. In many cultures, snakes and women alike have a radiant allure tinged with mystery and danger, as they may change at any moment and avenge the desecration of the land and the injuries done to their bodies and spirit. Soe Yu's work captures the menace of this metamorphosis and the fear it strikes deep in the hearts of men, a superstitious dread of the liminal bodies of beings with the power to create and destroy in the spaces between worlds of earth and spirit. Clay, as the originating material for the mythic bodies of primal snakes and women, shares their properties of plasticity and regeneration, so it flows under Soe Yu's hands in metamorphosis between one state and another. The sculpture is paused at the precise moment of flux when one body is turning into another, then it is fired and vitrified into a hard but brittle state, capturing the moment of change that inspires fear.

Soe Yu says the Serpent is a healer that emerges from

the dirt, which is why it features in so many symbols associated with medicine. Dirt is the source of life, but it is also considered unclean—a paradox that is projected onto both women and snakes. Her ceramic work signals the moment of dissonance at the heart of this paradox and seeks healing for the wounds of the earth and of women, while unsettling the totalising dogmas of autocracy and oppression that afflict her people.

All is not lost in Myanmar. The sacred Serpent is older than all religions, and in most multicultural modern nations there are still First Peoples present and folk customs that defy all efforts to suppress them. A good example of this in Myanmar is the festival of the Nat Kadow, which predates the arrival of Buddhism. For one week every year trans women are revered as 'Spirit Wives' and worshipped as they dance in the streets, while monks retreat to their pagodas and mutter about them being products of bad karma, and the ultra-conservative government turns a blind eye to the celebrations. Such are the minor victories that keep hope alive for marginal people existing under the belligerent glare of what we refer to in Aboriginal Australia as 'boss men'.

We call out here in solidarity with the many villages and tribes of Myanmar's 135 First Peoples who are fighting in jungles and city streets to overthrow the military dictatorship that has imposed years of brutal terror that we don't hear much about in Australia. They have regained a strong position, reclaiming many territories and cities for the people. Recent regime change in the US, however, has emboldened a lot of dictators globally, dismantling the interdependencies and soft power mechanisms that have disincentivised authoritarian expansion since World War Two. The growing enthusiasm worldwide for boss-man power means that the future of Myanmar's First Peoples is becoming increasingly precarious. The US withdrawal of humanitarian aid in early 2025 caused the shutdown of medical services and refugee camps, and we wonder what possible difference we are making by typing the word 'solidarity' above. All we can do to help is tell stories, knowing that narrative is more powerful than bombs if you wait long enough.

The Myanmar stories point us-two towards Indonesia and China, but we are heartsick and homesick, longing to move southward again. The Chinese Serpent has an unfamiliar name and a relationship with power and wealth that is alien to us, so we will go to Indonesia first, the last place we will visit where he is called Naga. It will be a moment of transition between Snake names and stories, because Indonesia also has hybridised Javanese and Chinese Dragons. So through our relationship with Naga we might receive an introduction to the Loong before we enter his realm, which is the right protocol to follow in our customs of travel. We've recognised the Dragon Queen too, which is a good thing to do. In the Age of Discovery, the protocol of 'Take me to your leader' usually meant 'Who's the man of the house here?'

EVE, THE SNAKE WOMAN

That didn't work out very well for the world, so we're glad we've checked in with the woman of the house first.

We will not find respite from authoritarianism in Indonesia, but we may find secret islands where Macassan smugglers once took shelter from European empires, continuing their ancient embassy and trade with Aboriginal Australia until the early 1900s. We have words in our Indigenous languages that they shared with us over centuries of good relation, and we still use some of those words in our house when we talk about things like seashells, dolphins and money. Us-two feel like we have safe passage there. We need this, because it is dangerous to follow the path of the Serpent without care and connection.

SCALES, WINGS AND CROWNS

We're sitting with our friend, the artist Dias Prabu, piecing together a shared story of ancient trade relations between Indonesia and Australia, a history of embassy disrupted only a century ago by colonists, but largely forgotten. The story has a lot of holes in it, but we are weaving new threads across the whole cloth of our common history with stories of Nagas, Javanese Dragons and Rainbow Snakes. A picture is emerging of how cultural exchange, wealth and innovation can flourish through trading practices based on mutual benefit and good relationships, rather than competition and avarice. There is nothing strategic about our treaties, and we have no need of tariffs or embargoes to protect our interests and rig the system in our favour. Our old borderwork protocols dictate that we create a compatible context of Lore before rushing into trade, Ceremony and innovation, so we begin by sharing our Serpent stories and images with Dias.

Well, strictly speaking, we talk a little about the Mad Max films before that, because we have all been to Broken Hill where those films were shot, and where Dias has exhibited his batik pieces as part of his efforts to re-establish the ancient embassy between our Peoples.

We talk about our connections with keepers of the Waawey Serpent story from the Darling River, and the Two-Snakes story that moves through the multi-tribal embassy site of Gundabooka near Bourke, then runs all the way out west to the Lower Darling River country, where the Serpent called Natji lives. Perhaps we should be telling stories about the history of copper mining there on Baakindji land, the industry that broke Broken Hill and is breaking Dias' own homeland as we speak. But Dias tells us about the Nagas in Indonesia, who are troubling for some of the more orthodox Muslims there but generally accepted into the daily customs of all. The Indonesian Naga resembles a Dragon, but it is legless and more serpent-like than the Chinese Loong, which is also present in the swirling theological pastiche of the region. The first Naga was called Antaboga, a bridge between the ancient Serpent Lore of Indonesia's First Peoples and the arrival of Hinduism.

SNAKE TALK

Antaboga has taken on some of the characteristics of Chinese Dragons since its early arrival, making it the prototype of what has become the Javanese Dragon. But in less populated Indigenous areas in the region there is no mention of Dragons or Nagas, only Snake entities. Snakes and mythical human-serpent hybrids appear in ancient cave art across the archipelago, painted up to 50,000 years ago. In those days, Homo floresiensis (a tiny hominid) and the Komodo dragon (a giant monitor lizard still in existence on some islands) walked side by side in Indonesia. Dias doesn't have any stories of those little people, although we do, but he tells us that the Snake belongs to the cultures of the Earth, and that its transformation into the Dragon is always an indicator of the arrival of kings.

He shows us images of his award-winning murals and massive batik art on fabrics up to 100 metres long. His themes are about the relationship between nature and Javanese tradition, translated in images of the Serpent as the protector of earth and sea, juxtaposed with the Chinese Dragon of wealth and good luck. They have many similarities, but the Javanese one has no legs and is wearing a crown.

He also shows us images of traditional weapons and instruments decorated with Serpents, Nagas and Dragons, including swords and daggers called krises. These are traditional weapons reserved for nobility. Today, people can only own those weapons if they have 'king energy'—the aura of a person of higher integrity than normal people. Makers

SCALES, WINGS AND CROWNS

will only craft Dragon krises for kingly folk—if you are an ordinary human and obtain one of these weapons through nefarious channels, it will break or be lost. There is a deeply programmed response in the background of our minds that says, 'I want one!' But we purge that thought, because it's not enough just to show respect—we have to feel it. We know there is not a regal bone in our bodies, so those krises are not for us. Oh, but they look so deadly!

Dias says the makers can search your spirit to forge a weapon suited to your energy, so most people will not possess a blade fashioned in the form of the Serpent. Krises are crafted only by a caste called the Pandes, who have the ability to read a person's energy from their ancestral bloodlines. The kris designs are differentiated according to caste, in the classes of priest, warrior, merchant and peasant. The caste system introduced by the Hindus is informal today, but still influential. It's illegal to exploit others using caste authority, but unwritten social conventions still prevail, including whom people are allowed to marry. Customs like these are always difficult to eradicate completely—but this cultural resilience also means whispers of Serpent Lore from the First Peoples continue to inflect Indonesian ways of being and knowing.

The Dragon and the Naga have retained more ancient Serpent identities as protectors of the earth and sea, notable in folk reactions to the floods and tsunamis of 2017 and 2018, which devastated coastal communities in Indonesia. Dias says that these catastrophic events made people intensely aware of their precarious position on the coastline. The cultural response to this insecurity has been a resurgence in respect for ancient ancestral entities and tradition. Customary dances, songs and stories were suddenly not just things to perform for tourists but were reinstated as Ceremony to protect the people from catastrophe. They recalled that the Dragon was not only a protector of the earth but of the ocean, and that the great Serpent is sometimes disposed to punish human behaviour with inundations, volcanic eruptions and earthquakes.

In Java, people say that if you have the Dragon in yourself, you have personal protection. He is carved into gates and doorways to ward off evil, even in tourist villas. He is often depicted with another entity of protection, the Garuda, who defends the sky while the Naga protects the land and sea. But the Javanese Dragon crosses all three elements, and is the ultimate symbol of security for Indonesian real estate. Dias portrays the Javanese Dragon with stars for eyes and the beak-like mouth of a bird, suggesting a spiritual fusion with the Garuda.

This relation between avian and serpentine beings is not unique to Indonesia. In our families there is a connection between carpet python and Goodithulla eagle totems, and in the Kulin Nations where we live and work, Bunjil the eagle created the land in partnership with his close relative, the Serpent. In many Semitic traditions the demonic figure

Dias Prabu's batik (tapestry) is a churn of Hindu Naga, Buddhist and hybrid Javanese Dragons with Antaboga Snake, linking to Indonesia's Indigenous traditions entangled across all time.

Mu-raay Djeripi walks us through a chain of historical events, visiting the Dreamtime of both the Celts and Aboriginal Australia then on to fifteenth century Ireland and seventeenth century Australia. Two ancient peoples joined by both invasion and spirit and now blood.

Mu-raay Djeripi shows the Kabul carpet python creation being, moving out from its sacred increase site in four directions.

Sun Loong on parade in Bendigo in Australia's goldfields, where dragon culture was kept alive during the repressive years of China's cultural revolution.

Women offering money to Naga Snakes at a pagoda in Myanmar.

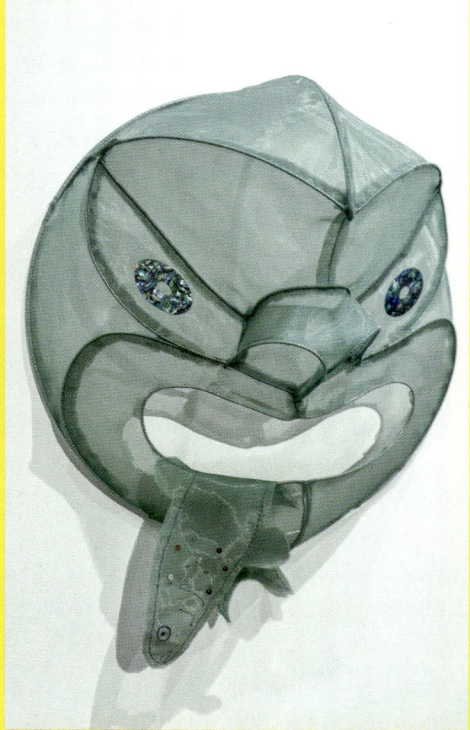

Clockwise from top left:

Andile Dyalvane's non-traditional ceramic form has been channelled by the serpent deity, emerging from the coiled base as if it is rising up from a rock. This reflects the re-birth and re-surfacing of identity that was erased by the oppressors.

Soe Yu Nwe's ceramics draw on the fluid quality of the snake's body to reflect on the transgressive nature of femininity. This piece hybridises Nuwa (the Serpent woman) and Naga Maedaw (the Burmese dragon queen).

Though normally a wood carver, Ngaroma Riley used the more ephemeral material of organza to depict the guardian Taniwha (Māori water spirit), reflecting its fraught status in the face of urbanisation.

The dragon embraces the serpent on Ultimo Road in Haymarket, Sydney. Mural by Jason Wing and Maddie Gibbs.

Tyson Yunkaporta's bark shield with Serpent pattern, alongside Megan Kelleher's she-oak fighting stick, to keep us safe. Also a Rainbow Snake sculpture (representing all the Snake Talk stories from round the world), along with all the traditional tools that Tyson made specifically to craft these things.

of Lilith (Adam's first wife, who was cast out for not obeying her husband) has the traits of both birds and snakes, sometimes appearing as an owl and sometimes as 'the tortuous serpent' who tempted Eve. Bird, Serpent and Woman are often entwined in Lore and there are neolithic figures found around the world of women with both avian and serpentine features.

The Bird is creation and the Snake is destruction, while the woman is the sacred embodiment of both. This trinity often represents realms of heaven, earth and the underworld, particularly in European traditions, where women bridge the worlds above and below, with womb and tomb symbolically unified as a site of birth, death and rebirth. Reptiles shed skin and birds moult feathers, while both lay eggs—common traits that have always inspired a genealogical relation between them in human stories of evolution and creation. They are paired in love and war across the massive canon of Phoenix Lore from Egypt, Europe and Asia, while elsewhere they are even embodied as a single hybrid entity.

Serpent beings are often described as having feathers and wings, like Quetzalcoatl in Mesoamerica, whose name literally means 'bird-snake'. Old Lore always holds Bird and Snake in a relationship of tension and balance between earth and sky, sometimes in conflict and sometimes in harmony, and we have found this story everywhere we have travelled. Even Anishinaabe First Peoples in Canada have shared Lore with us about Thunderbirds in the sky who struggle with horned Serpents on the earth, in a similar relationship to that of the Hindu Garudas and Nagas.

The Garuda is the logo of Indonesia, a symbol of power and control of the skies, and it has a troubling relationship with the Naga in Hindu traditions, as the warlike mount of Vishnu who spends eternity killing Serpents in search of the enlightened condition of 'ultimate release'. The Garuda carries the potion of immortality we have previously encountered in stories of Lakshmi, the goddess of wealth. But this relation is softened in Indonesian Lore; for example, in many weddings, the bride represents the sacred Bird while the husband represents the Dragon. In Java the Garuda is not just a powerful protector from the sky but also represents peace and calm on earth. There are different nuances about the Garuda and the Naga in Sumatra, Java and Bali, as diverse as the Lore from Thailand and India. But Dias prefers to see the Dragon and the Garuda in a collaborative relation.

All this complexity is the result of involuntary, unregulated cultural embassy, but Dias seeks to return to a more stable historical protocol of exchange, which is why he uses his art to signal the reinstatement of ancient relationships between Indonesia and Australian Aboriginal communities. He invokes treaties that existed from the sixteenth century until the nineteenth century, when goods traded along the Silk Road from as far afield as Europe and China made their way into Java, Sumatra and Macao. From there, the Silk Road continued into Australia's north. When the Dutch East India Company arrived and the colonisation of what would become Indonesia began, Dias says there was a tiny island in the Selayar archipelago where Asian traders would hide from the European invaders and store their cargo, before risking the crossing to the Banda Islands and the north coast of Australia. On those islands there were horrendous massacres perpetrated to control the spice trade, and the trade of goods between Indigenous peoples became covert, illegal smuggling.

Macassan traders had long established an embassy with Aboriginal Australia, under a tamarind tree that was planted on Yolngu land, whose tasty fruit was introduced to the continent and became a naturalised species over centuries of biotic and economic exchange.

The Wik language spoken in our own household contains many loan words from Indonesia, including remat and otamat for periwinkle shells and dolphins. Wukal, our word for money, predates European colonisation and probably came from Indonesia as well. In the Gulf country of northern Australia, naga is the word for loin cloth—the same as for peoples in North India and Myanmar, and in many Hindu traditions across South Asia. Other Aboriginal languages in the centre of our continent also use this term, and many tribes from north to south have traditionally worn the red fabric loincloths acquired through the trade of textiles and other exotic goods from abroad, long before European explorers landed on our beaches. We know that this trade existed before the sixteenth century treaties, however, as our only placental native mammal, the dingo, was introduced from Asia thousands of years ago.

Indigenous Australian borderwork has influenced international embassy protocols for a long time, well before the Westphalian system of sovereign recognition arrived on the scene. That new tradition of borderwork did not facilitate good relations, from our point of view. As we have encountered in popular stories about the 'pirate's code', the European Treaty of Westphalia in 1648 was more like guidelines than a strict set of rules, and some sovereignties were more respected than others, depending on how much those with the firepower wanted something beyond their borders. Nothing much has changed, in that sense.

Dias is seeking to reconnect the old embassy system, not just for trade, but for communication of sacred knowledge as well. There was a massive financial crisis in this part of the world early last century, after the Australian government stopped the trade between Indonesia and Aboriginal Australia, in response to the 'Yellow Peril' moral panic of the day. The White Australia Policy escalated exclusionary borderwork practices and quarantine policies based on fear and hatred. Anti-Asian propaganda was spread among northern Aboriginal communities, and was later expanded during World War Two with fears of Japanese invasion, especially after the bombing of Darwin in 1942.

The Aboriginal communities along the north coast of Australia were conscripted as a first line of defence against the fleets of invaders who were imagined to be soon descending upon this white colonial outpost on blackfellas' land at the bottom of Asia. Our own relatives were forced by missionaries into panicked marriages, with warnings that if young women were not married, they would be raped by Asians. This has left a legacy of racism in Aboriginal communities that lasts to this day. We still have family members who refuse to be in the same room as mee' many (little eye) people. So, even in our own families, Dias's message of ancient embassy now seems foreign and strange.

Reinstating the old borderwork protocols from a century ago seems an impossible dream in a time of post-colonialism in Indonesia and neo-colonialism in Australia. During the era of decolonisation from 1945 to 1960, independence was selectively granted to nations according to criteria we have not yet been able to discover. Perhaps it was only offered to those whose traditional dress involved covering the torso with fabric. For whatever reason, our First Peoples missed out on sovereignty at that time, leaving us hopelessly out of step with Indonesia. This meant we did not have a voice when the Global South was trying to make sense of itself after World War Two, which is a shame because we would have given Asia and Africa some sage advice—two simple rules that might have saved the world a lot of pain in the decades of horror that followed.

1. If you have a meeting that Europeans are not invited to, make sure they don't know about it.
2. Never make Europeans feel like they have done the wrong thing, because they will punish you for that forever.

Indonesia made the mistake of hosting the 1955 Bandung Conference, at which the leaders of newly decolonised nations in Africa, Asia and the Middle East gathered in embassy to discuss the future of the hemisphere. Their focus on addressing global inequality and the ongoing devastation of their lands and Peoples raised alarms in the Global North, where there were concerns that these ideas were too 'left leaning'. The critique of oppressive western power stung the USA and Australia in particular, as both countries were doggedly resisting civil rights movements at home and did not appreciate 'inferior' nations attempting to overtake their progress in the development of human rights. There was also concern that democracy and liberty in southern nations might impede the capacity of the Global North to strip them of their natural resources and exploit them for cheap labour. The backlash was swift and severe. Wars, massacres, corporate land theft, assassinations and the installing of brutal dictatorships and puppet governments followed, on an apocalyptic scale that made the Bandung delegates wish they had never set foot in Indonesia.

Australia played a significant role in the military

interventions of this punitive campaign, resulting in the installation of a murderous autocratic regime in Indonesia that was amenable to foreign corporate exploitation. The regime lasted until the end of the millennium, but the foreign stranglehold remains. Australian tourists continue to enjoy holidays that are cheaper than travelling in Australia—an experience of imperial nostalgia complete with non-white servants and universal deference. An international airline named after the sacred Garuda provides a steady stream of entitled tourists seeking wild jungle adventures, pristine beaches, exotic trinkets, two-dollar massages, cheap alcohol, child prostitutes and hair braids.

All the while, foreign mining companies continue the same reckless copper extraction that devastated Broken Hill—the Australian ghost town where Dias exhibited his work in honour of the trade that once existed between Indonesia and our Indigenous Peoples. But the Natji, the Baakindji Rainbow Serpent who resides there, has now been in communion with the Naga, the Javanese Dragon and the Chinese Dragon through Dias's artwork. As mere humans facing the geopolitical and historical barriers of a global system that is eating us alive, we may not be able to do much to recover healthy international relationships. But the First Peoples of the Lower Darling region who live in Broken Hill believe that the Natji can travel the world beneath the earth and sea, popping up in bodies of water as distant as Loch Ness in Scotland, communing with his Serpent relatives everywhere. His cousins rest in the fossilised bones of plesiosaurs that can be found in Antarctica, Russia, Asia, America, Africa and New Zealand, and he likes to join in with family reunions from time to time.

What would it take to follow our Serpent ambassadors and overcome the iron borders and politics of hate that divide us from each other and threaten our survival? The answer might be found in the amazing story of the Chinese Dragons that have made their home in the goldfields of Australia, among some of the most resilient, patient and forgiving people on earth.

It might seem strange that we're not going to the source in mainland China, but the continuity of Dragon Lore was maintained by Chinese emigrants throughout the twentieth century, so we follow the Loong now along the winding paths of diaspora. Also, the only member of our family who ever went to China is a dark-skinned sister who said they were always rubbing her arms and face to see if the black would come off, and the whole family lost enthusiasm for travelling to visit the Great Wall after that.

There are ghosts in our historical imaginations of China, from recent encounters with their mining companies to the legacy of anti-Asian propaganda in northern Australian Aboriginal missions during World War Two. There are shadows of attraction and repulsion in our hearts that are irrational and complicated, cast there by the lies of some fairly shitty people. This is a troubled relation that

SCALES, WINGS AND CROWNS

needs our attention, and we've decided to start that work with the Chinese communities living on Aboriginal land, who face many of the same forms of hostility that we do.

Also, our Serpents have already met.

DRAGONS UNDER THE SOUTHERN CROSS

When we were kids, we were told that our people used to eat the Chinese because we liked the taste of their flesh. Us-two grew up moving between rural and remote areas in either historic mining areas or lawless construction camps around new mining sites, where such revisionist histories were always doggedly plastered across the origin myths of settlement. We recall urban legends divined from human bones exhumed in modern mining operations, which employed advanced technology to siphon the scraps of gold remaining in old claims from the gold rush that began in 1851. These were dismissed as 'Chinamen's bones' to save on the cultural heritage paperwork that is involved in disturbing Aboriginal remains.

The bones were said to be the remnants of cannibal feasts, but it is difficult to imagine how we might have managed such culinary abominations in the middle of a bustling, angry throng of miners jealously guarding their claims, or in the sprawl of hastily erected towns with more pubs than houses, where we were not welcome (with the exception of our women, who were kept for recreational purposes). We were openly exterminated, or removed from those places, while the Chinese were loathed but tolerated, and often 'disappeared' with the blunt explanation that 'the Aborigines must have eaten them'. All the while, the bones of our slain, which were scattered everywhere in the bush in those days, were tramped into the mud.

Us-two have spent a lot of time walking over the old diggings of the goldfields on Taungurung Country in Victoria. We have stepped across the haphazard networks of earth walls thrown up to channel water to the mining claims, where the ground is pock-marked with tiny ponds when the water table is high. It is difficult to tell whether the holes were made by miners, or by pastoralists and timber cutters removing old-growth trees. The scars in the landscape reveal historical layers of boom and bust in various industries, including logging, mining, sheep farming and the military development and testing of explosive, chemical and biological weapons.

SNAKE TALK

Sometimes you can find birthing trees, or trees hollowed out for the production of smoked eel meat, which the Taungurung once traded near and far. There are stone tools on the ground where meat ants swarm over their mounds, constantly rearranging tiny white, red and black pebbles to signal changes in the weather, as they work to keep the temperature constant in their nests. Black snakes chase marsupial mice and there are green branches lying on the ground under the young trees, cleanly severed as if by sharp steel tools. The beaks of eagles have made those cuts, and they have left the branches on the ground to dry out and use later in their huge nests. The eagle is called Bunjil here, and Bunjil is the Creator who flies high and sees all.

In these lands, the Creator controls the movement of the Serpent, whose name is Mindye. He lives in areas rich in quartz crystal, the mineral that contains most of Australia's gold. Bunjil surveils the activities of people, and if they fail to follow the Law in sex, marriage, Ceremony, killing, or the treatment of land and children, then he will send Mindye out to punish them with his pestilent breath, which infects all with deadly diseases.

During the gold rush, miners took part in the destruction of sacred sites, massacres, the devastation of forests, grasslands and waterways, and the sex trafficking of Aboriginal women and children. In their squalid camps and haphazard towns, they were plagued by smallpox, typhoid, dysentery, scarlet fever, measles and cholera. Perhaps these epidemics were visited on them by Mindye, or maybe they were just a result of the common settler practice of dumping sewage into the same waterways they drank from—a habit that continued well into the twentieth century.

The Chinese enjoyed much better health, though, as they brought doctors with them to the goldfields and kept abundant vegetable gardens, both of which they generously shared with any European miners who didn't completely reject these things as heathen devilry. Say what you will about Chinese herbal medicine; it was a better option than putting leeches on your genitals and taking handfuls of mercury pills. And, of course, if you wanted to 'chase the Dragon', there was always an opium tent available in the Chinese camps, where you could forget all about your missing teeth and rotting feet, while your relatives fought in horrific wars abroad to control the opium trade, and your dreams disappeared into muddy ditches. The ashes from your opium pipe would be collected and given to Aboriginal indentured labourers, incarcerated on reserves and pastoral stations, to keep them docile and dependent.

The Chinese outcompeted the other miners in the goldfields because they were healthier, cleaner, better organised and more cooperative. They had clan-based systems of mutual aid in which they pooled their mining claims, shared tools and organised their labour. They took on claims that were deemed exhausted by others, digging deeper and further down, in circles rather than squares. (If you've ever dug a grave, you'll know that corners are bastards of things to maintain once you are past waist-height.) The Chinese were bitterly resented for their success and their communitarian values, which ran counter to the competitive ethos of the colony.

Everybody else was looking for the individual jackpot, working for themselves, cheating and fighting each other, not bathing for months as they squabbled and schemed in the mud. And here were these 'Celestials' walking immaculately across all of it, making a fortune! The anger and resentment this caused added fuel to the moral panic of the 'Yellow Peril', which inspired the White Australia Policy as the unifying principle of Australian Federation in 1901. Still, the Chinese community continued their patient efforts at diplomacy, parading imperial dragons in the streets of Melbourne during the Federation celebrations. While this did promote a degree of tolerance and grudging respect, the panic endures today, under the new slogan of 'Asian invasion!'—although stories about this in mainstream media have died down over the last decade with the prioritisation of anti-Islamic sentiment. Despite persistent racial hostility, Chinese Australians are thriving today. Many are still managing wealth, businesses and property in extended family groups rather than as individuals, and they continue to operate an internal welfare economy in their communities.

It's not all blossoms and rainbows, though. There is still human trafficking and exploitation of Asian labour here for migrants who don't have citizenship, as occurs in every rich colony when settler birthrates don't keep pace with economic growth. A carefully maintained 'border crisis' provides a permanent, precarious underclass to prop up the nation's standard of living. Outrage-bait propaganda ensures that the very existence of migrants is criminalised in the popular imagination. They are demonised for 'free riding' on welfare, while paying taxes to a hostile state and doing the worst jobs in the most dangerous conditions to lower the cost of production, with limited access to government benefits. They provide cheap cleaning and childcare options for new parents who have to return to the workforce after their brief maternity or paternity leave is finished. Collectively, they also have a vital role as a punching bag for politicians shouting about imaginary open-border policies. These demagogues throw raw meat to disgruntled settlers who need someone other than their daughters to provide the cheap hand-jobs available in Asian massage joints, which can be found in most Australian cities.

There are complexities here at the overlap of many cultures, histories and grievances, including our own. Many narrative paths weave through the story, and we can't tell it alone because our maps are incomplete and we are damaged and angry, so we need a friend who can act as a diplomat for us in this fraught territory of lies and terrible truths. Billy Potts, who has acted as an interpreter and enabler in the relationship between the Australian Chinese community and master Dragon makers in Hong Kong, is perfect for the role. He is the son of English and Chinese parents who sees himself as an intermediary between cultures, making esoteric and folk knowledge accessible to the world. He says that Serpents and Dragons are liminal, sitting in a space between spirit and material realities, which inspires him to see his status as both insider and outsider as a gift, allowing him to be an informal ambassador.

We share Lore together as we come into relation. We tell him about our family's role as custodians for a sacred site called Moving Stone, where there is a rock that stands in a different place every time you visit. We can't camp there because there are thaypan everywhere—that is our word for the deadly snake that Australians have renamed taipan, the Chinese word for 'big boss'. It is also our word for the Rainbow Serpent, who lives at our sacred site. In our stories the sacred stone travelled to this continent in a whirlwind from China, and our old people often describe mythical beings dwelling at Moving Stone that look like fu dogs.

Billy tells us about the nature of sacred Dragons, the colourful ones that feature in street parades. He says they are not created by people but are pre-existing entities of spirit that become embodied through the collective skill of artisans and performers. They are never referred to as 'it' or treated as inanimate objects. They are mostly male, because the female counterpart in spirit is the Phoenix, who has her own customs and Ceremony. Their forms are incorporated into architecture to bring good luck and wealth, and their lines of travel are accommodated in urban planning. He shows us examples of an architectural feature known as a Dragon's Gate, a giant hole through the middle of a tall building that allows Dragons to move between mountains and sea without being thrown off course by skyscrapers.

He tells us the story of the Dragon Mother, a human widow from an ancient fishing village. She has no children, but one day finds some beautiful round rocks on the beach that turn out to be Dragon eggs. She takes them home, they hatch, then she raises the infant reptiles as her own children. This of course diverts us to a sidetrack of speculation about *Game of Thrones*, the hugely successful books and TV shows that might have been inspired by this story.

He also tells us about the Fire Dragon Ceremony, which begins with villagers finding a giant python eating their livestock, so they kill it. Soon there is a plague, and the people realise they have actually killed the Ocean Dragon's son, so they create an annual Ceremony to appease the entity and cleanse the land of sickness. Still today, they make a plain, skeletal Dragon out of rope, straw and bamboo, bristling with smoking joss sticks, to parade through the town and down to the beach, to immerse in the water where the Dragon lives. This old tale echoes some of our own Indigenous stories, in which the coastal Python entity is the slain son of the Rainbow Serpent. These stories contain calendars that have always indicated the right times for cleansing smoke Ceremonies and for burning undergrowth to regenerate the land.

Then Billy tells us a newer story, of the imperial parading Dragons that emerged from the historic gold-mining towns of Victoria, like Ballarat and Bendigo. There are three in Bendigo: Loong, Sun Loong and Dai Gum Loong. Loong literally means Dragon. Sun Loong means New Dragon, and Dai Gum Loong means Big Golden Dragon. Sun Loong was the longest imperial dragon in the world, until Dai Gum Loong was created in 2019, measuring 125 metres. The oldest of the three is Loong, who was made in the Guangdong Province in the Qing Dynasty, the last dynasty of China. In 1901 it was shipped to Victoria at great expense, by the Chinese who were living in Bendigo.

They ordered the Dragon not just to celebrate their own traditions, but to make themselves visible, and to reconcile with a European settler community that was extremely hostile towards them. Billy says the unique Australian Dragons exist because of this hostility, as the people wanted the violence against them to stop and called on the power of these mighty entities from afar. Their spectacle and inherent charisma are compelling, and the Chinese community used their dramatic allure to find their way into the hearts of the European locals. They collected donations from the crowd at the parades, touring the Dragons across Victoria, with the proceeds going to the building of hospitals.

Loong is delicate now and very difficult to parade.

They paraded him for the first time in many years in 2019, at the Easter parade in Bendigo. The people carrying him wore white gloves, and each had a little bag so that if a piece fell off they could pick it up and keep it for restoration work after the parade.

We ask Billy why Australia has such record-breaking Dragons. He says it all comes down to climate and historical fate. Victoria is mild and dry, unlike much of China, where the humidity makes the Dragons decompose quickly, so after a few years they are traditionally burned to return their spirit to the sky. As for the history, the precarity of Chinese settlers during the goldrush and the White Australia Policy might have caused them to cling to the protection of their Dragons and traditions. Later, the communist revolution in China outlawed a lot of traditional practices so aggressively that even the racist hostility of Australia provided a relatively safe haven for the imperial Dragons.

The CCP established the Republic of China in 1949. Under the new regime the Bendigo Chinese couldn't go back to Guangdong to restore the damaged Loong in his birthplace. In the late sixties, the harsh policies of the Cultural Revolution were suppressing Chinese folk tradition, so the Dragon makers moved to Hong Kong to keep their culture alive. Later, when this enclave of specialists was established and thriving, the Golden Dragon Museum was built in Bendigo and delegates travelled to Hong Kong with the dream of making the longest Dragon on earth.

There are many records and firsts with Chinese Australian Dragons. When Dai Gum Loong debuted in 2019, it was the first time in history that women were permitted to participate in the carrying of the Dragon. This caused quite a stir in the Bendigo community. Billy says, 'Dragons can bring out the best in people but also bring out the worst.' They are the bringers of wealth, so there is often squabbling over who can carry the Dragon, and a lot of political manoeuvring. The inclusion of women upset a few of the men who were worried about losing face, but Billy describes the conflict as the beginning of a new kind of cultural revolution, one that was creative rather than destructive. It transformed the culture of both Chinese and European settlers.

When Dai Gum Loong joined the Easter parade, he became a symbol of collective effort and genuinely democratic purpose, of accomplished men and women moving together as one. The Easter parade in Bendigo used to be about hats—ostentatious headpieces crafted by settler ladies as a symbol of personal status and exceptionalism, and worn in competition for a prize. Today the festival is about collective joy and losing yourself in a riot of colour and spectacle, where everybody wins.

All things great and terrible in this world are about symbols. Symbols are powerful things that can maintain cultural continuity—or even mutate beneficially as collective folk responses to change—but they can also destroy. Billy talks about the way ancestral symbols of land and people can be destructively co-opted into the service of power-hungry individuals and elite special-interest groups. He offers both the mafia and the Communist Party as examples of this.

The triads who run organised crime in Hong Kong tattoo the sacred image of the Dragon all over their bodies, not for peace and good luck, but to harness the power of the Serpent and signal, 'Don't mess with me! I will destroy you!' Billy perceives similar motivations in the depiction of the modern Chinese nation, government and economy as 'The Dragon', which he feels is a profane co-opting of folk culture and traditional spirituality by a powerful elite who almost destroyed that culture. He says the meaning of the Loong has been twisted into a perverted signal of aggression and dominance that plays on western religious fears of the Serpent as a menacing agent of evil. 'The CCP is no friend to Chinese culture. The CCP is only a friend to itself. They are now burying the fact that they almost destroyed this culture entirely.'

We respond that it is the same in Australia with the symbol of the Southern Cross, a sacred constellation in our Aboriginal cultures. Only senior Aboriginal people in very secret rituals can reproduce its image, which must be erased immediately afterwards as it is too sacred to be present in mundane life. Yet it is featured on the Australian flag along with a miniature British flag, above a seven-pointed star representing the states and territories. The Southern Cross is also depicted on the Eureka flag, which for some people has become the equivalent of the Confederate flag in the US (and not just because it includes a cross made of stars). It is now tattooed on Australian bodies as a symbol of white supremacy for anti-immigration activists and is especially popular with neo-Nazi groups.

The Eureka Rebellion of 1854 is regarded by white nationalists as a milestone in the formation of the Immigration Restriction Act and the White Australia Policy, which were central to Australia's Federation in 1901 and the birth of the nation. The famous battle at the Eureka Stockade is Australia's version of the Boston Tea Party in America. It is usually told as a story of gold miners staging a revolt against British rule, giving rise to independence, labour unions and democracy. The rebellion opposed unfair taxation laws, but it was sparked by escalating hatred and violence against Chinese miners. The conflict was resolved when the rebels were appeased with decreased taxation for white miners and the introduction of Asian immigration restrictions, along with punitive taxation and exorbitant tariffs on Chinese imports. And, thus, the identity of a nation (well, a federation of white Christian ethno-states owned by a monarch on the other side of the world) was born.

The Chinese community have continued their incredibly patient efforts at making cultural embassy with white Australia, even erecting a monument to honour the fallen rebels who persecuted their relatives—a gesture that we find difficult to understand. We do, however, appreciate a more recent gesture that was a little cheekier. The Golden Dragon Museum commissioned a master flag-maker in Hong Kong to create a new Southern Cross parade banner, featuring the Chinese characters for culture, people, peace and righteousness. Billy says this was about reclaiming the constellation from white supremacists, countering the bad energy and neutralising the hatred.

We often think of diaspora in terms of dispossession and loss of culture. But perhaps it is more like a time capsule, or the doomsday seed bank scientists have established on the arctic island of Spitsbergen. Even European migrants who have formed ethnic enclaves in Australia have managed to preserve cultural practices and dialects that no longer exist in Europe. If you want to know how Calabrian was spoken a century ago, for example, you only have to visit Mildura on the Murray River. As for China, its complicated history over the last century meant that a lot of folklore in the homeland was lost, but much of it was preserved in Australia, Singapore, Malaysia, Taiwan and Hong Kong.

Hong Kong is a particularly diverse collection of cultural seed banks, even for European culture. There are aspects of old England that exist nowhere else but there, such as sheriff's offices that collect parking fees, and a unique ginger drink from the days when the British owned India. But the most exciting site of cultural preservation there is also the most innovative, and that is the discipline of Chinese lion dancing and drumming, which is thriving because of its strong relationships with enclaves of cultural exiles around the world. When lion dance drummers died out in mainland China, they thrived elsewhere, not only preserving the tradition but innovating new rhythms with Polynesian influences from cultural embassy with Hawai'i and Honolulu. In Australia and America, the lion dancing is more dynamic and athletic than the traditional forms, so today every international competition team seeks Hawai'ian, American and Australian Chinese artists to create the most spectacular performances.

Most of the revitalised folk culture in the world is the result of humans finding refuge in the hospitality of strangers and making it happen. As scholars we might hesitate to attribute this to the connective spirit of the Serpent, because there is no evidence of this being a real phenomenon. But as Indigenous people we feel the presence of entities like Mindye and Natji in our travels, making kin with Nagas and Dragons. Even if they aren't real, the new lines of kinship certainly are.

Here is where we take a bold step and suggest that recovering authentic cultures of profound connection through Serpent Law is potentially possible for everybody. Separation from homelands and the eradication of many cultures makes this difficult, however, so we will need to discover a process of cultural recovery that can survive forced removal and ethnocide. For this, we will go to Africa. There are Snake People there who know how to recover the lost cultures of the earth in their dreams.

HAVE SNAKE, WILL TRAVEL

To be Aboriginal in modern Australia is to be an alien in your own land, to be constantly claiming sovereignty but never being sovereign, to be continually decolonising without the possibility of a post-colonial future. Like our Native American cousins, we missed the era of decolonisation when Europe partially divested itself of stolen lands in Africa, Asia and South America, so the occupation of our Country will continue until the continent becomes uninhabitable. Us-two often wonder what our people would do if Australia became truly decolonised, if we faced the same circumstances as the people we have met on our travels so far, in places like Myanmar, Indonesia, Mexico and India. Would we simply re-colonise ourselves as an aspiring developed nation, as so many Third World former colonies have done, or would we recover more sustainable borderwork practices by revitalising the Law of the Serpent?

We're not the only ones here who are sick of colonisation. There are growing numbers of European settlers who also long to decolonise and return to a more satisfying and sustainable way of living (although most imagine this Utopia as a place where they can still retain the wealth and status they have inherited from their murderous forebears). They feel a genuine sense of grief over the loss of their own ancestors' traditional knowledge and Ceremony, yearning to recover authentic lifeways and connection with the land.

We seek answers to these concerns in post-Apartheid South Africa, a decolonised nation with aspirations of wealth and development, where our Xhosa friend Andile Dyalvane lives in Cape Town and works to revitalise his culture after centuries of brutal dispossession. Luckily, his clan is descended from the sacred Serpent, and as we have found in our journey around the world so far, the spirit of the Snake never dies.

We introduce ourselves by naming our clans, lands and totems—a protocol which Andile says brings him joy in a world where many of these things have been lost. He reciprocates with his own customs of introduction, involving recitation of 'praises' listing his family's genealogy connecting back to a Serpent ancestor, the ooJola that is the totem connected to his Nkwankwa clan name. He admits he has not always had access to this knowledge, which is something his community has worked hard to retrieve over the last few decades.

His clan originally came from a village on the Eastern Cape but was forcibly removed to prison camps when their land was stolen. Later the survivors migrated to the city. They were converted to Christianity, so their old customs were forbidden, and no written records were ever made of their former ritual practices and spiritual beliefs. It seems like a hopeless scenario—with all the historical dispossession and the unstoppable trajectory of South Africa's industrial development, how can it be possible to recover a land-based spiritual tradition and way of life? Andile says the answer lies with ooJola, the Serpent. He even asserts that if Elon Musk ever manages to colonise Mars and sends his clan there to mine emeralds, they will still be able to connect with Serpent spirit and recover their culture of origin through collective spiritual practice, even if they are light years away from home.

Andile says that when you travel in time and space there are no boundaries, so your physical location does not prevent you from being spiritually located in ritual sites of meaning. For him, the spirit of the ooJola offers a methodology for cultural inquiry, so it doesn't matter how much cultural content and information you lose, as long as you retain the process for recovering and adapting knowledge through spirit. This process involves hearing whispers and dreams from the ancestors, then submitting these for analysis by Elders with all the community as witnesses. Everybody has different cultural vocations as makers, musicians, dancers and so forth, so everybody carries those spiritual messages into their work in preparation for Ceremony. After the Ceremony, the connection is increased and each person in their vocation is open to more whispers from the ancients, which are shared with all in ways that gradually cohere into cultural narratives and customs that have ancestral continuity in spirit. This process of collective meaning-making cannot be co-opted by any particular person to form malevolent cults. The Elders ensure that people who have been chosen for spiritual roles do not get carried away and start imposing their own agendas on the collective.

Andile is a chosen person in his clan, as one who can receive intense visions and messages from ooJola and the ancestors. The role comes with a lot of obligations and no perks, but he inherited it from his father, a Christian who set aside half his faith for traditional practices involving honouring and sharing dreams as sacred signals. This Serpent-dreaming process of inquiry was difficult to enact in his father's generation, with the punitive dogma installed by missionaries insisting that any encounter with Snakes (either in dreams or daily life) was a visit from the Devil, a poisonous evil that carried bad portents and warnings of enemies nearby, requiring defensiveness and vigilance.

His father found Serpent dreams even in the oppression of city life in the Apartheid regime, as well as the degraded lands around the city that were overgrazed and sparse, where animals were dying in vast numbers. During the upheaval of the struggle for independence, many fences were torn down and boundaries opened, allowing access to more land. Amidst the chaotic flourishing of vegetation reclaiming desolate neighbourhoods and landscapes, his dreams grew stronger. On his death, he passed the role of dreamer to Andile, along with the understanding that the Serpent is a blessing, not a curse, and that it demands your attention and action. It is not a personal spirit guide, but a group identity woven into your lineage and community that must be shared and worked with collectively.

Andile tells us how the ooJola and the ancestors whisper to people like him in dreams, revealing vivid images of different kinds of gatherings and Ceremonies, plant medicines, structural designs, animal knowledge and the names of things long forgotten. The Elders analyse these for internal cohesion with known patterns of Lore and etymology. The dreamer's role is to create spaces of meaning that allow people to listen and rediscover ways of appeasing and honouring the spirit of ancestors and places in the land. We understand this, having experienced similar altered states in deep sleep, or induced by ritual, or during powerful events such as the birth of our children. Andile adds that the ooJola often appears to his people during childbirth, a visitation that is regarded as an act of blessing or anointing the child. It also often appears when a journey must be undertaken or a fateful decision made, communicating approval or disapproval with words, looks, emotions and movement. He does not share our experience of seeing through the eyes of our totem animals during these visions, however, saying that his people avoid even looking at the ooJola's eyes.

Apart from his role as a seer, Andile also works as we do in the crafting of cultural objects for spiritual inquiry, connection and meaning-making. But where we use wood, stone and fibre, he channels symbols and forms through clay to communicate and document messages from spirit. He works with clay from the Eastern Cape, which makes him feel closer to home because the smell of it reminds him of the first rains and the river water near the village of his old people. When he can't source that, he uses generic terracotta mixed with a little clay he has personally collected from his river, twelve hours' drive away. That was the place where he used to play and work as a child, where he first encountered the whispers of the ooJola. He always keeps some of that clay in his workspace to spark the informatic tendrils that bridge worlds like the tree roots in the riverbank, which he feels in the clay and running through his hands when he touches it. 'I touch clay and it's all these receptors attached to the ancestors; all biotic life emerging from the mud.' But this is not automatic—none of it works without a lot of preparatory protocols and discipline.

HAVE SNAKE, WILL TRAVEL

He cannot make something from his own imagination or desire, because the clay will not move for him and the Serpent will not emerge. He must be in an altered state, in which the forms and designs of spirit are not coming from him, but through the clay, from land and ancestors. He prepares for this by walking in the mountains and wild places, then using traditional herbs and specific foods that will clear his spirit and allow the Serpent to bring unclouded visions. In the city, mountain walks are not always practical, so he keeps a sacred space for offerings in his workshop for burning herbs and dried cow dung, which not only cleanses the spiritual energy of a place but also repels mosquitoes.

These indoor offering spaces have been maintained as a secretive practice for centuries, as they were forbidden in colonial times. But these days people share them publicly, near the front of the building by an open door that is welcoming of passing strangers who may smell the fragrant smoke and come inside to sit with them, feeling the ancestral energy and spirit together.

Andile shows us three clay sculptures revealing different aspects of ooJola, called Qengeba, Ngwanya and Nkwankwa. He pays homage to the spirit of his totem in three gradual stages, the seed of the message as it is whispered, the affirmation of the message finding its rightful place with his people, and the remembrance of who they are in a repositioned reality beyond displacement. The startling discovery he made in this instance of inquiry was that the

SNAKE TALK

Serpent spirit of their homelands was *displaced with them*. It was not left behind but travelled with the people to their new location! This might be unsurprising to folk who follow the great religions of empire (who are used to uprooted deities becoming universal creators), but for us it is surprising to hear about the native entity of a sacred site uprooting itself and moving to the city.

But we know the Serpent likes to migrate seasonally and even visit new places from time to time, so we trust that this emergent Lore is coherent within Indigenous knowledge systems. We can also tell that Andile is the real deal, that his work is not a performance or a bid for eyeball hours on the web. His work is always grounded in traditional protocol and subjected to community review. He knows that if he or any of his peers are doing wrong, then everyone suffers, and as one who is chosen to channel ancestral messages, he is obligated to sing them and pass them on. He is not permitted to interpret them and present them for praise, as western artists do. His work must be interpreted by the people, who can then determine what needs to be done. He describes it as a trust that is kept by the entire clan, governed collectively as knowledge that must be distributed.

Us-two appreciate this from our cultural point of view. We might perform spectacles of arts and literature for an anonymous public, using the fragments of knowledge we are allowed to share—but the deep knowledge is held in our community, and we can't claim that individually. If we find it and try to keep it for ourselves, we will get sick. Andile concurs: if he ever tries to keep his ooJola revelations to himself, he will be punished. He might become ill or something might go wrong in his work. He is surrounded in his practice by a lot of people in different disciplines, like song makers, instrument makers, artists and keepers of traditional language and custom. Each person is called to follow these complimentary vocations, and they all hear the whispers of the ooJola and the ancestors.

They undergo rites of passage to gain the ability to heal their family and clan in communion with each other, with the place, and with the entity of the Serpent. They receive the guidance to change and move together in adaptive traditions, and Andile suspects that this is probably the secret of the cultural success of the African diaspora. Everywhere that African migrants travel, they innovate ingenious responses to new environments and conditions. Wherever they land, their traditions undergo a dynamic, shapeshifting embassy within the culture, place and spirit of their new home, in dialogue with the ancestral entities that they bring with them.

Networks of specialists in Andile's community working with sound, writing, rhythms, art, music and song engage together with nature and healing in the certainty that the spirit of the Serpent is inside them. 'The spirit of the Serpent does not perish; it lives amongst us and can endure and reincarnate a primal intelligence with truth. It goes out from different places, follows the people, lives in ancestral lines rather than places.'

Andile says that ooJola migrated to the north Congo with his people thousands of years ago, then followed them back when they returned. He tells a history of his clan walking in the path of the Serpent and navigating the politics of all the clans that came to be known, collectively, as the Xhosa, managing land and adapting through various upheavals. It is a very different story from what we have read of savage tribes in eternal wars, enslaving each other until they encountered the British, who tried, in peaceful coexistence, to help them organise themselves until the Dutch Boers took over that mission, working tirelessly to establish 'separate but equal' self-determination for the ungrateful and violent natives (who presumably had no arts or crafts apart from some simple beadwork).

We're more inclined to share Andile's oral history, which has been revealed through ancestral spiritual practice, rather than recycle this written narrative, because Andile's history has the benefit of rigorous peer-review. We also think it is a good Dreaming for the Anthropocene, an era in which climate change will displace billions, creating massive itinerant populations. It will help to have portable totemic entities of place that can migrate with the people and help sustain cultural vigour. Andile says that in their traditions of journeying, his people maintain connection with the Serpent by staying attentive to the environment and elements all around, frequently stopping to acknowledge beautiful plants or grasses encountered on the trail, speaking to the entities of each place and leaving offerings, then meditating on how far they will travel with the memory of what they have seen.

Andile has made embassy in this way all around the world. He once visited Maine in the US to connect with the spirit of the Serpent on Wabanaki land. The Elders hosted and feasted him like a long-lost relative, holding Ceremony for him and giving him the name of Dancing Moon, because the ancestors had called him there so that all who have suffered together may rise together. They said Andile would shine for them whenever they saw the moon, because that is the spirit of his people.

We don't have the same poetry and rhetorical panache as our Native American cousins. We never quite know what to say or where to look when Polynesians, Africans, Indians, Mayans and others start orating like this at international gatherings. If you ever catch us talking like that, we're probably pulling your leg (or trying desperately to fit in). We're as superstitious as most humans are, but we're far too practical and shy for grand speeches invoking big spirit and prophetic visions of great consequence. Andile is quite good at it, though, and he has passed on a message for us to give to you:

> *Keep singing, keep singing. It doesn't matter what you forget or is disrupted, it is still coming through your dreams, and it will still gather you together and make those ceremonies happen through you. That can never be stopped.*

DEADLY WYRMS

We have been making embassy with Lore-keepers in Ireland for a couple of years now. We have family connections there through the Kellehers of Knockraheen in County Cork and all their descendants in Australia, as there is a strong tradition in our land of Irish marrying into Aboriginal families. Some say the word didgeridoo is a Gaelic word, but there is still debate over that. Certainly, Australian Rules football was invented when Aboriginal and Irish people bonded over their traditional ball games (and a shared hatred of the British). Also, we all like to say the word 'deadly' a lot. Both cultures share a history of ancient trade with Asia and the transmission of ancestral Lore through oral tradition—there have been artifacts from Asia found in Ireland that are up to a thousand years old, and the Irish carry DNA from stone-age First Peoples who lived there at least six thousand years ago. This leads many Irish to believe that their Lore (which is very different from other Celtic cultures) may have been passed down from that time. This theory of cultural continuity is supported by the evidence of ancient stories still told today, which include observations of the ice sheet that once covered Ireland melting around ten thousand years ago.

We have been having yarns and setting up exchanges between our cultures with Irish natives Manchán Magan and Lydia Campbell, who both live in the countryside near Dublin. This relationship has been part of our lives for long enough to share Serpent stories at a deep level of knowledge, with patience and caution to avoid setting off any earthquakes or floods in our eagerness to bring our songlines and ley lines together. When Manchán visited Australia recently, we introduced him to Uncle Noel Nannup in Perth to share his Celtic Serpent Lore and learn about Waagal, the Rainbow Snake from Nyoongar Boodjar. They found many commonalities, especially around cultural understandings of waterways. We also introduced Manchán and Lydia to each other, and then to our friend Mu-raay Djeripi, who travelled to Ireland and stayed with them for a few weeks, where they shared Lore and Ceremony.

Our Serpent yarns were delayed for a while by children

and exhaustion, then by severe storms in Ireland that knocked out the power and wifi, but now we're finally seeing each other's faces on our computer screens across wildly disparate time zones, laughing and enjoying a bit of cheeky talk, or what the Irish call craic. Manchán is a folk scholar, and Lydia is completing a doctorate about Irish traditions. They are both practitioners of spiritual rites and customs passed down or retrieved from ancient times. Much of Manchán's work is grounded in expert historical knowledge and research, while Lydia tends to be more intuitive as she allows her body to flow through the rhythms, stories and cycles of the land. Manchán says it is important to work in this experiential way, and through yarns, because most of the Lore has not been recorded in print. While much was written about the culture by priests, this often twisted the old stories to suit Christian morality and imperial schemes. He says the absence of Irish Elders in written history and anthropology is largely intentional, a self-imposed silence to protect potent and sacred knowledge that can only be passed on 'from knee to knee', from grandparents to grandchildren across generations. The Lore-keepers did not die out—they were driven underground over centuries of invasions by Vikings and the English, and they took refuge in the west of Ireland, where they quietly preserved their traditional knowledge in secrecy.

Surprisingly, Manchán says their 'knee to knee' knowledge was also threatened by the Druids long before that, whom he describes as a patriarchal cult that sought exclusive dominion of spiritual knowledge to maintain the power of an elite, priestly caste. This shatters our historical misconception that the demise of the Druids signalled the passing of the old ways into the mists of time, and that St Patrick banished all Serpent entities and Lore from Ireland in the fifth century.

Manchán tells us about two Serpent beings, the Wyrm and the Great Wyrm. The Wyrm is present in most bodies of fresh water, and frequently travels the waterways and beneath ground, moving between Ireland's three thousand wells and springs. Lydia affirms that these holy sources of water are the vaginal openings of the matron of the earth, reflected in the native words for every kind of surface water, which are named after female reproductive organs. Caves, coves, estuaries, gullies are all named this way, along with many landforms that are categorised as breasts, pregnant bellies, thighs and fecund loins. Seasonal Ceremonies are still held at many sacred wells, where people await the arrival of eels, which are regarded as manifestations of the Wyrm and his blessing. Manchán reflects that in both our cultures there are narratives cautioning careful approach and even avoidance of this realm, particularly for children. The Irish Lore is stricter than ours, though, with traditional custom preventing all people from learning how to swim.

Lydia says the Wyrm is a protector of the sacred feminine and of the 'earth medicine' healing Lore that gives humans sovereignty over their own health and wellbeing. Manchán adds that this still exists in fragments, explaining a treatment called the Wyrm knot, which is still practised today. A complicated knot representing the Wyrm's tortured body is made with a string or rope, then placed over the afflicted area, and if it is made properly it comes undone when both ends are tugged, pulling the illness from the patient. Lydia describes the systematic eradication of folk medicine and herbal knowledge as a dismembering of human life and nature through the conquest of Woman and Snake. Today, the Serpent is still present in medical symbols such as the caduceus, but is always bound up in these images with rods and staffs as weapons used to slay and control him.

Manchán argues that the old people were not innocent of those crimes either—there are tales of Irish folk heroes battling Serpents too. But they were chiefs, princes and kings, and if we've learned one thing in our journeys it's this: across the world, monarchies are always founded on the destruction of the Snake, the ancient enemy of men who seek power over others and control of feminine flows in the land. The Snake's presence has endured from the time before kings, a constant protector of the land which is a sentient matriarchal being. We can see echoes of his continuity in neolithic Irish petroglyphs and cave paintings, as well as in serpentine stone monuments at burial sites that are still regarded as places of transformation and regeneration today—Lydia says, 'They are wombs, not tombs.'

DEADLY WYRMS

Manchán and Lydia both share stories of the Hag, a hideous crone who, according to the Lore, has existed since the days when the sea between Ireland and England was still a forest. She gave birth to the most sacred sites in the land by dropping stones from beneath her apron. The heroes of the ancient tales attacked her as well as the Wyrms. 'Just like St Patrick, they're all the fucking same,' Manchán mutters. As they set out on this quest, the heroes were cautioned that, when they slew her, they should be careful not to stab her in the thighs, as this would cause a cataclysm, but of course they did not heed the warning. A giant Wyrm emerged from a cut on her thigh and wreaked havoc, eating people and tearing up the countryside before sliding into a lake. The Hag's power and size increased to massive proportions and she began snatching up people and livestock to throw into the lake to feed the Wyrm.

The Hag represents the realm that lies beneath the ground and water, which is the home of the Wyrm. They both often emerge and move across the surface, then into the air, spanning the three layers of the world that are connected by the Celtic tree of life. Lydia says that we humans also perform the same function as the tree, channelling energy across those realms as we care for creation. When we are severed from this role, creation falls into chaos, and we are cut into pieces. The work of re-membering our amputated parts is the work of the body in ritual, when we become the tree, the Hag and the Wyrm and unify the realms.

SNAKE TALK

She tells another story of the Hag that has helped her in this work, a tale of five brothers sent to hunt a mythical white stag to determine which one of them will be chosen to inherit their father's kingdom. They are halted by the Hag in her most putrid form, and she will not let them pass. She asks for a kiss in exchange for access to the stag. Four of the brothers, who are the legitimate heirs to the throne, refuse in their pride and disgust, but their little bastard brother is humble and has nothing to lose, so he generously offers to kiss the Hag and even lie with her. He is not just 'taking one for the team' in this selfless act—he genuinely sets aside all feelings of revulsion and gives himself completely to her. Then she transforms into a beautiful goddess who rewards him with the stag and the crown.

Lydia recalls when she participated in a Ceremony celebrating this story. Immediately afterwards she felt as if she was dropping into another world, where she experienced two hours of vivid visions. She found herself in a fouled and decrepit house, where she was compelled to stay but prevented from cleaning up the mess. She had to overcome her disgust and be at peace there, before passing into a deep underground cavern and then a beautiful valley. The message was 'Love me as I am, and I'll give you everything.' She realised that people cannot experience transformation and return to the old ways through Ceremony until they first sit with the 'bones and rot' of their existence, accepting the vile truth of what they have become in modernity and then letting it go. Avoidance of this hard rite of passage is the reason new-age spiritualists fail to recover their ancestral connection to land and Lore—they engage in spiritual bypass and dwell in ecstatic loops of shallow ritual, profaning the hard path of authentically intuitive practice.

The Hag's name is Cailleach, and she is similar to the Hindu goddess Kali, who often has a vile appearance and rules over the death and destruction that must precede new beginnings. Cailleach governs the season of winter in the same regenerative role, and Manchán has a whole theory and body of work around such links between ancient Ireland and India, but we won't share it here because there are too many Nazis who misuse these ideas as a validation of bullshit Aryan identities. They've read the same theory in *Mein Kampf* and the conclusions they draw from it don't exactly have a good historical track record of improving the world. Their engagement with Celtic and Nordic folklore tends to be very selective, always skipping the parts about honouring the sacred feminine, embracing strangers and caring for the land. They can read about it in Manchán's books if they like and steal some more sacred symbols to tattoo on their stinking hides (although we know it would kill Manchán to see that).

Manchán says the terrifying nature of the deep and hidden realms belonging to the Wyrm and the Hag is an integral part of the old Law, as it places limits on the excesses of men who are obsessed with power and supremacy. The

Cailleach rages with storms and destruction, bringing death in winter but shape-shifting into the goddess Brigit in spring and summer. If men are grounded in their traditional roles, then this transformation inspires awe rather than fear of women and land, keeping human communities in balance. Women have the role of descending into the darkness during the worst days of winter and into the deep places of the earth where men cannot follow, retaining power over birth and death where humans dwell. The famous Shannon River is a reminder of this Law, as it was formed by a Wyrm that was banished by heroes reacting to their fear of Woman and Snake. Manchán refers to the river as an 'elongated piece of knowledge and enlightenment' placed there by the Serpent. This is what us-two would call a songline in our culture.

Lydia concludes our yarns by explaining that the dwelling places of the Serpent lie in the west, which is the direction that corresponds with autumn in the Irish equivalent of the Native American medicine-wheel philosophy. It is a season of calm before the chaos of Cailleach descends with winter, and the Wyrms abide there, consciously facing death and moving deliberately towards it. She also talks about the wooden pendant she once gave us, featuring an Ogham symbol associated with springtime. She knows we have faced more than our share of death and despair in the last few years and could use a glimpse of Brigit's face and a new beginning.

It's time for another dramatic change of scene, then. How about some mountains and jungles?

SERPENT BRIDGES

Making kin and enriching relationships is work that must be done. It does not need to serve any particular purpose, because the work is an end in itself—it enlivens creation, promotes increase and sparks complexity. There is a lot more to it than full body hugs, sharing personal trauma stories and doing deep breathing exercises, however. We see many people doing those things while throwing around words like 'kin-making' and 'Ceremony'. Proper Indigenous principles for making kin, making embassy and doing Ceremony are more rigorous, and we have found these practices everywhere in the world, from Africa to Ireland

and everywhere in between.

In Indigenous embassy we must bring our entire spirit with integrity, and we have to take time to show each other we are complete and whole before proceeding. In this testing period, if there are disturbances or sickness in spirit with any of us, we must help and heal each other before we proceed. If the disturbance can't be resolved, the afflicted person needs to step back. The inclusion of non-Indigenous people in these spaces is difficult—even if they are spiritually complete as individuals, they are usually embedded in spiritually incomplete traditions and communities. Either that, or their spiritual integrity has made them strangers and outcasts in their own families and cultures, leaving them wounded and isolated. Your collective relations are part of your spirit, and if you are missing this part then you are like a living ghost. Many of our own people have this problem, and it usually means they don't know when to step back, so Ceremony just stalls and fails when they are present. This happens often, so it is always wonderful when you find people who are complete and who know what they're doing.

Our family is connected in embassy this way on every continent but Antarctica. Here, we will share some of the things we have learned in embassy with Cañari and Kara::Kichwa people of the Andes::Amazon. (Our friends like to use double colons instead of slashes in their punctuation.) Those lands in Ecuador are home to an entity called Amaru. Like every Serpent we have encountered, he was not made by the Creator but predates the universe, a being of the deep dark who existed before creation as a vast, slumbering potentiality. He made tunnels and bridges between worlds as a dualistic being who assisted with the formation of the cosmos, sometimes with conflict and sometimes with connection. Within us, he makes the bridges between the parts of our spirit that must be joined and whole before we can enter the altered states of Ceremony. Us-two have begun moving in and out of these ritual states with Amaru's people, and we can share some of that process here, because it is something that Indigenous people feel and know together but have seldom thought about how to explain to others in procedural terms. But we have thought explicitly and deeply about this together, and how we might translate it for others who are trying to come home.

Firstly, we must be sharing Lore when we are moving towards Ceremony together—this is where our differences become familiar and provide the ground for complementary purpose to emerge. We connect macro-narratives about shared entities like constellations visible from both homelands, and knowledge of the similar flora and fauna or migratory species that already connect our places biologically. The Serpent usually provides pathways for exchange, as an entity in myriad forms embodying the unique spirit of each place, offering the key for feeling our way into cross-cultural immersion. Gift exchange is important at this stage. We trade significant items that embody the depth of knowledge and degree of obligation we are committing to the relationship. These are sentient objects that will migrate with us and reside with our families to maintain the presence of our new kin and keep us linked in spirit.

Ceremonial Indigenous embassy is not the same as our social borderwork customs of seeking passage, access and permission—in those situations we are coming alongside with requests and agendas such as 'We want to hunt in your territory this season', or 'We want our grandchildren to learn from your net-makers'. These are usually long-established relationships that are already integrated with the symbiotic flows between bioregions. Embassy Ceremonies, on the other hand, are usually the result of novel encounters. These emerge from lawful voyaging outside of regular migratory routes and can be initiated by both humans and non-humans. Crows are a good example of voyagers who facilitate embassy. They are problem-solvers and can adapt their habits quickly, and those changes create signals in biological networks that trigger shifts in plant and animal behaviour or relationships. They can be messengers that amplify the adaptive patterns of Ceremony to signal changes we are making in carefully designed 'natural' systems such as forests.

Humans and non-humans often voyage together, and this can result in creative or destructive disruptions in the places they visit, depending on whether proper protocol is observed. The observance of protocol is the responsibility of the visitor as well as the host. Encounters from lawful voyaging are voluntary and involve mutual consent. Other novel encounters can be involuntary but still lawful, in situations of displacement or evacuation as the result of invasion or natural disaster. Non-human fellow travellers in all these cases need to be managed as they gradually adapt to the habitat, and the habitat adapts around it in response.

When the voyaging is unlawful, however, when there is no mutual consent or common protocols and the visitors' actions are invasive, then non-human passengers are not ambassadors or refugees, but victims of trafficking. When they enter a new ecosystem without human stewardship, they enact destructive behaviours as a trauma response and cause a lot of problems. When a new species is trafficked in this way, retroactive embassy must be enacted to bring it into right relation and balanced symbiosis. Extermination is not an appropriate or effective response, and we do not think of these species in terms of contagion, pollution or toxicity.

Often, we will hear the call of new species who wish to come under our care and Law, or the more distant call of our own species that have been trafficked abroad. We heard the local call of the poisonous cane toad introduced here from South America decades ago, making sure it had a song, story, totemic category and a dance, with Ceremony teaching the watchful crows how to avoid the poison and eat the belly, then the crow, in turn, teaching other species how to do this too. We have recently heard the international call of our eucalyptus trees that have been trafficked to the other side of the world, where the cane toads come from. This call needs to be answered and there is much work to be done, because most of the eucalypts in the world no longer grow on our continent.

We have done some Ceremony and exchanged gifts with Kichwa people here and offshore, initially coming together under shared Lore of constellations that are visible in the night skies of both countries, and which both our Peoples call the Seven Sisters and the Hunter. Our engagement in this process has overlapped with several yarns and shared projects with Nkwi Flores, who is a Kara::Kichwa scholar and ritual adept who works locally to preserve traditional ecological knowledge and Andean philosophy.

Nkwi has shared with us how his people have worked with Australian gum trees that have been trafficked to Ecuador by colonists over the last two centuries. The First Peoples have carefully managed the trees to become part of the bio-cultural system and an important part of traditional medicine, Ceremony and the crafting of ritual objects. In our worldview the trees are sentient beings, and collectively they are a totemic entity that both our cultures now share. That is the entity that has called us together.

Other entities are brought in to enrich the relational space between us and the ancestral circles around us, including Orion and Pleiades, tobacco, cane toad, crow, chocolate and waterlily. We've learned to take the chocolate seriously—that is a very sacred entity for Andean people and works powerfully on your body and spirit. Colours are also entities, and we are working with red, white and yellow so far. Elements too: earth, air and water, but mainly water as the most sacred conduit of spirit for our peoples. This is the element our Serpents work through to weave all these entities together with eucalyptus spirit in our ritual exchanges, and that is the yarn with Nkwi that we will share here.

Amaruk is the name of the snake as an animal, and of all Serpent knowledge and wisdom. Amaru is the name for the cosmic entity of the Serpent, what Nkwi classifies in translation as a 'BioKreaTure'. Amaru is of the underworld, the unconscious depths of the land and people. The land is sentient, and so it has a psychology—the surface is *Hanan*, the personality and character; the sky is *Hanank*, which is like the ego and superego; the subterranean world is *Uhku*, which is like the subconscious; and finally there is *Uhrin*, the unconscious, the deep dark of the cosmos. That is where Amaru lives, and when you do Ceremony, you have to enter that space while still remaining conscious, which is quite a feat. The 'testing' part of our protocols (both in Ecuador and Australia) is where we make sure we can prepare everyone present for this crossover. Our Serpents test us. Amaru is the checker, the verifier, the maker of endings and new beginnings. And that is his wisdom—knowing when things should begin, and when things should end.

The image of Amaru looks like an infinity symbol, but

in the elaborate diamond and zigzag patterning of Andean aesthetics. In the centre of the symbol, you are dying and being born, celebrating and mourning. Two heads of the Serpent emerge, symbolising the duality of the warlike feathered Serpent in his season and the nurturing scaled Snake during the planting and harvest season.

In the season of nurturance, Amaru in reptile form moves in his infinity symbol loops that increase until they cover the land. Every part of that shape has intersections and spaces and curves that show different complementary energies and entanglements, informing the mathematical patterning of the sorting and arrangement of seeds and the planting designs in the fields and on the slopes. Companion plant relations are woven into the design, with the timing of all fruiting, flowering, seeding and dying in different species' rhythms coordinated like clockwork. Woven fabrics expressing these patterns have been exchanged between Kichwa women and our family, containing more knowledge than we could write in a hundred books.

Amaru is the balance between opposites, the duality of all things. Even an infinity Serpent can't stay in a figure-of-eight loop forever without falling apart—eventually it will need to be disrupted, turned over and begun again. So the martial face of the Amaru emerges from the warrior dance Ceremony that is performed during the summer solstice, in which he transforms into a feathered serpent. Here he takes to the sky, to inhabit the psychological ego of the earth. The warriors both call him and follow him there, dancing in curving lines and undulating columns, moving like the water and the wind, which is conceived as a zigzag pattern in Andean symbology. Nkwi sings the song, and the repeated chant of the war formation in one word, which translates as 'Swing swing swing!' This expresses the diagonal, back-and-forth advance of the ranks, embodying the motion of the feathered Serpent as warrior.

Amaru provides the wisdom to help people hold themselves within a concept of reciprocity that is not conceived as a karmic transaction of equal benefit for givers and receivers. It is a misconception that Indigenous economies demand reciprocity in an equal return of effort or items of value to individuals. There is no ledger but there is an accounting in the balance between the concepts of Aini and Mashinti. These are bafflingly complex codes that require the wisdom of Amaru to calculate how things are distributed in collectives and natural systems, when no individual's efforts are rewarded over another's.

Imagine being spectacularly talented and working your butt off for land and community (Aini), while your silly cousin drinks wine and sleeps all day. Why do you-two both enjoy the same benefits of abundance? Where is your reward? Why isn't he punished? What is wrong with this system (Mashinti) that distributes the outcomes of every exchange throughout nature in ways that only Amaru can comprehend?

Aini is about caring for things, making offerings. If this is your investment of energy and wealth, then Amaru is your portfolio manager. It all goes through his calculations, his 'wisdom checking', and you never get an individual return on investment. What is offered goes to the system of land and people that cares for you, and if that system does well then you are enriched.

But so is your no-good cousin, fuck it! You might feel that an injustice has been done, so then you fly up into *Hanank*, the realm of ego. Oh! This is bad. If Amaru follows you here, it is hard for him to return, and no good can come from him being trapped here. Mashinti is the governance, the morality and grounded ways of Indigenous living systems. Amaru gives the bigger picture of how things are maintained and what your place is, why in one moment you are giving all without expectation of personal return, but across all the moments of your life you receive far more back from the system in which you live.

Nkwi worries that our Indigenous communities are so often losing touch with our own nature. In ourselves we have *Uhku* and *Uhrin*, the underground emotions and dark side we cannot see, but we do not live there. We live in *Hanan*, which is our intersubjective persona, our collective thinking, feeling and being in community. It is who we are in this world. But then there is *Hanank*, where we have our heads in the sky, caught up in ego and superego. It doesn't matter if we are in our highest self or shittiest self up there—it is not a place to make camp. When you go in there completely, the bridge is gone, and you stay trapped in your own narcissistic hell. *Hanan* and *Hanank* are supposed to be joined so you can return, but the bridge disappears when you are in *Hanan* too long, and then it starts disappearing across the other four realms too, and not just for you—you are connected to everybody else. See now, that relational karma cuts both ways, doesn't it?

The Kichwa name for those four-dimensional bridges is *kinray*. The Serpent uses them to travel between realms, and as humans we use them inside of ourselves to unify the four parts of our own spirit::being, so we can become entire people who are capable of moving into the primal void of *Uhrin*, the deep unconscious of the world. This is the unique altered state of Ceremony, when we can enter that realm consciously. That is when we can sit down with the land as a sentient entity, and with the Serpent, to diagnose problems in the ecosystem and move in spirit to weave the right patterns and motions in dance to trigger the responses that will heal.

You are not special in this, and you are never alone. Even your relationships do not stand alone, because every connection needs a connector. So every relation is a triple alliance, with a *kinray* in the middle as a sentient third party. Amaru is the one who can bridge all worlds, from the bottom to the top, because *Uhrin* in the deep must balance the peaks of *Hanank*, or lands and communities fall apart. This trinity is embodied in the 'three sisters' of Andean crops. Corn is the *kinray* for the bean vine to climb up towards *Hanank*, like the Serpent, and then the squash grows in *Hanan*, the collective reality of our sustained habitat. This is a pattern woven into Andean fabrics and painted and carved in both sacred and mundane objects. We were going to say 'ritual objects' but everything, every bucket and blanket used in their lives, is sacred and decorated with the patterns of Law and Ceremony. As we have seen, this even extends to punctuation.

Pondering Nkwi's use of the double colon :: in writing, as a symbol of connection to replace the forward slash / as a symbol of division, we may find extra layers of meaning in the concept of *kinray*. In maths, the double colon usually indicates a ratio in which both values are equal, and in the computer coding language known as Python it is used to connect things to categories. In logic it is used to combine symbols in analogies, representing the 'as' part of ideas like 'hot is to cold as up is to down' (hot:cold::up:down). Thinking about *kinray* as a bridge, in light of the double colon in Aini::Mashinti, we don't see the two concepts as a pair to consider in isolation, but as entities connected to other reconciled dualities and relationships. The horrendous complexity contained in the casual statement 'All things are connected', becomes apparent when you sit within Indigenous cosmologies, so it is helpful to have Serpent Law as an accounting system to sort through your relational receipts and keep things in balance across all the layers of your existence.

It is wonderful to live in cultures of such profound relatedness, but then there is always that devastating moment each day when you are confronted by the fact that this is no longer the reality for all the people, that the world is falling apart, and many are lost. Nkwi says this is because Amaru is being broken down into different parts. The warrior ritual has been used to inspire marches, protests and actions to reclaim urban areas for crops and Ceremony, but power and control systems are unending and there is always more resistance required. The warrior spirit of the feathered Serpent is not able to return to the water after its season, remaining in a permanent state of war. New generations have been taken away and trained in the military, returning with a very different vision of an Amaru who is out of balance, represented by a new version of his sacred symbol that looks more like a swastika than an infinity symbol. The Snake is broken into many parts, not only in the winter soldier's perennial quest for freedom, but in priestly crusades for control.

As a beloved entity providing guidance, strength and compassion, Amaru was co-opted in Ecuador by Catholic missionaries, who incorporated the Serpent in church services and religious art in a kind of spiritual transference. They provided a safe space for people to practise Amaru rituals, but then merged these with the gospel, where they gradually dissolved, assimilating the people into the new system under one god. They neutralised resistance to colonisation by connecting their imperial deity to the Indigenous totemic system, while undermining that system and eventually replacing it in the governance of land and people.

Nkwi talks about the common vulnerabilities and strengths of our Aboriginal and Andean totemic systems, in particular the way they tie everyone and everything together to form pluriversal networks of diverse stories. Many narratives may contradict each other, but they cohere to form the fabric of creation, with each story coming into focus in its proper place::time (or, if you want to get pedantic, space:place::time:season). This is the collective reality of the *Hanan* realm, which Nkwi translates as 'intersubjectivity'. He says the Christian faith-based system is the opposite of this, a totalising subjectivity demanding that all stories be consumed and metabolised into one truth in a universal space/time mythology. In Andean philosophy it is accepted that you will make mistakes, and the Serpent offers the wisdom to make these disruptions generate increase in the self-organising, self-correcting weave of creation. The Christian approach by comparison is to condemn, correct or forgive under the authority of powerful men chosen by God to shepherd us towards apocalypse.

Nkwi's community is home to many passionate converts, Indigenous evangelists who reframe the Serpent as temptation. They induct new initiates by reasoning that Amaru is traditionally a representation of wisdom, which identifies him as the serpent in the garden of Eden who held all the knowledge of the world. The Serpent is the evil one in the biblical stories, who tempts us to gain knowledge and become wise, and it is wisdom that makes us do bad things. It is surprising how often this sequence of fallacious logic works, turning people away from their own traditional knowledge as well as knowledge of the world, achieving bliss through wilful ignorance and the unification of all thought into one story.

Unfortunately, those of us who keep the old ways and assert our Law can also become insular in exactly the same way, retreating into parochialism and aggressively policing our borders. This is when embassy dies, when we fight fire with fire, but if we don't do this we are burnt out and destroyed. The demand-sharing economies in our Indigenous systems of distributed abundance do not fare well in predatory marketplaces. They become pyramid schemes in which people of integrity sacrifice everything to keep the community fed and sheltered, while the benefit of this effort is co-opted by a handful of the very worst people and the majority succumb to apathy and despair.

Change-makers, 're-wilding' devotees and dreamers with alternative economy start-ups should heed the experience of Indigenous people struggling (and failing) to maintain traditional systems within global systems of capital. They would be wise to avoid investing in alternative financial schemes supposedly based on Indigenous principles (and there are hundreds of these), unless they want to lose their houses and nest eggs to some golden dragon's multi-level marketing scam. Hot tip: in capitalism there is always a yield, and if you can't see where that return on investment is coming from, then it is coming from you. Follow the Snake by all means, but mistrust snake-oil salesmen. Do not leap before the net appears—better to wait for the moment we can all take the leap together, rather than sacrificing financial security in futile gestures of virtue.

Collective action has always failed in modernity, however, because in every revolution the most ruthless bastards still end up rising to the top to build new pyramids on the rubble of the old. So how can we recover widespread trust and trustworthiness simultaneously, so we might safely rebuild interdependent, regenerative systems in the path of the Snake? Warlords and prophets demand that we convert or die, and we comply because we know that if we don't, the powerful will escalate their wars of vengeance against us. There are mean, angry bastards everywhere and we have to figure out how to deal with them.

Well, if it must be war, then we'll need to make an alliance with the deadliest warriors around. Let's meet some Viking Dragons.

RIGHT DESTRUCTION, WRONG DESTRUCTION

We will have some Viking yarns here, but first we need to do some thinking about the global epidemic of mean, angry bastards, to figure out the difference between the regenerative destruction of the Serpent and the terminal tantrums of narcissists. The distinction is important, because you can't speak truth to change the hearts and minds of people who lack the capacity for true love and thought. The cultural recovery efforts of Scandinavians might shed some light on this topic, but we will begin with a story a little closer to home.

There is an Aboriginal storybook called *The Rainbow*

Serpent that has been read in almost every Australian primary school classroom for decades—a Serpent story that most have probably encountered but do not remember in any meaningful detail. It is kind of disturbing out of context (and every school approaches Indigenous knowledge out of context). It is a story about Goorialla, a Rainbow Serpent from Cape York, as told by Dick Roughsey. He was a Lardil man from Mornington Island, where a lot of our family has married or been adopted into the community and culture. He passed away in 1985, but his story still sits uneasily as 'inclusive content' in Australian schools. Without understanding the Lore about creation and destruction, millions of Australian kids have carried away a sense of the Serpent as an abusive parent who gives with one hand and delivers arbitrary punishment with the other. They already get enough of such tyrannical deities in their churches, mosques and synagogues; they don't need to have it reinforced in 'Dreamtime stories' as well!

The principles of destruction in the Serpent Lore can be easily understood. Wrong destruction is a violent act that reduces diversity and complexity, in order to make relationships uniform, harsh and controllable by a supreme group or a powerful individual. This creates scarcity and dependence by limiting access to resources, safety, comfort and space to exist. Right destruction is a violent act that disrupts this state of affairs to increase diversity and plentiful resources. This is the work of the Serpent everywhere in the world, and an understanding of these principles could go a long way towards demystifying 'acts of God' and the 'mysterious ways' of many deities (although it would not be popular with those who use the power of their god to dominate in politics and business).

In the Goorialla story, the Serpent entity cared for the people and taught them Ceremony and the Law. But at that time humans and dogs were the dominant species in a flat, unchanging landscape of scarcity and monotony. Some creative destruction was needed, and it takes a deep-time perspective to make sense of the regenerative catastrophe that followed. But children with no Lore have a hard time understanding why a benevolent being would suddenly start eating people in that perfectly ordered paradise and changing them into parrots in his belly, then smashing up the huge mountain that was the only feature in the landscape, showering everything in stones the size of small hills, killing people to transform them into all the birds and animals of the most biodiverse natural system on the planet. It feels like abuse to them, so the story becomes a trauma trigger for a legion of horrors experienced at the hands of school bullies, dysfunctional parents and Aussie heroes with a hellish mix of empathy disorders.

People and entities with the markers of empathy deficit, borderline personality and narcissistic personality disorders populate all our old stories—they have been with us since the dawn of creation. Sometimes the Serpent kills them, but more often they kill the Serpent. Either way, because he exists across all of time, the moment of his death can occur at any point and not be an ending, because he is still present in every other moment that was or will be. So he just gets on with his timeless business in the everywhen, trying to offset the wrong destruction of narcissistic beings and create complexity from the stagnant order they impose. He works with broad brushstrokes, though; flood, wind, storm and sickness don't take care of the details, which are left for us to manage. We're supposed to keep his Law and manage the disruptions of the empathy-deficient from moment to moment. He has scaled up his work in recent years, but we are struggling to keep pace with him in an era when narcissism isn't an anomaly, but the norm.

Empathy has begun to feel like a disability in the cut-throat cultures of our world. The deep-time machinations of Serpents will eventually take care of the problem, but how the hell do we cope with the agony and fatigue of living in disordered systems in the meantime? The bullies aren't outliers anymore—they are in charge. They have taken over our workplaces, tribes and families, bringing coercion and cruelty into every area of our lives. It would be bearable if they could be satisfied with total compliance, like in the good old days of empire, but they don't want that anymore. They want to torture us and take our dignity, to consume our spirit of relatedness. They keep us close with the cruel tether of our hope that we can help them if we just

RIGHT DESTRUCTION, WRONG DESTRUCTION

try a little harder to please them. They want to see us die in despair or kill ourselves when our empathy is finally too scrambled and raw to bear—but they never attempt suicide themselves, because they are already dead.

In our Lore, we understand that these bastards are missing part of their spirit. They have committed a trespass in a sacred place, or violated the Law, or an evil person has done something to take the spirit out of them. They are incomplete, and hunger so much for the spirit they have lost that they must take it from others, but they are never satiated. They are living ghosts dreaming of immortality and they cannot be healed—even psychologists agree with us in this, with most asserting that narcissists are 'resistant to treatment' at best, and untreatable at worst. They have a scarcity mindset that makes them see any benefit for others as a loss of benefit for themselves. If you make time for yourself to do something, they feel like you have stolen that time from them. If you do good work, they feel like you have unfairly beaten them in a competition. If you speak freely, they think you are taking away their right to free speech. They long to be adored and respected by their society, while simultaneously wishing to destroy it. They weaponise the rules of that society against others, while considering themselves above those same rules. Their failures and shortcomings are always somebody else's fault. They scramble every sequence of logic to create dysphoria in their victims and ensure they escape consequences for their every act and utterance, remaining unaccountable even to their own chaotic internal reasoning. You might recognise the pattern of their destructive strategy in the following workplace dialogue:

> Sue: Nobody respects property anymore. Can you explain why all the pens are missing?
>
> You: Ah. Hello, Sue. Yeah, they're on the table there from the—
>
> Sue: Are you even concerned about theft? Because I'm very concerned about theft!
>
> You: Um, well the pens are just over—
>
> Sue: Why are you avoiding the question?
>
> You: Okay, well, what was the—
>
> Sue: Oh my god. I'm not engaging with this right now until you've calmed down. Please move out of my personal space.
>
> You: But this is my desk!
>
> Sue: Lower your voice, please! Talk to me later when you have calmed down.
>
> You: Huh? Ah, okay, I don't have any concerns but I'm free after one if—
>
> Sue: You just interrupted me. Again.
>
> You: Was I?
>
> Sue: Why are you being so defensive?
>
> You: Sorry, how?

RIGHT DESTRUCTION, WRONG DESTRUCTION

Sue: If you will just listen for a minute for once instead of constantly interrupting and trying to avoid the question! You're so defensive.

You: What was the?

Sue: You always do this. Everyone is concerned about this behaviour. I simply came over here because I needed a pen, and you started ranting and being abusive.

You: The pens are over there, where you put them for the meeting.

Sue: Oh, so now you're accusing me of being a thief?

You: No, you just put them there for—

Sue: What time was that?

You: I don't know…

Sue: Very convenient.

You: Well, the meeting was at twelve, so I guess five minutes before that—

Sue: No, it was at 12:15.

You: Okay, at 12:15—

Sue: So now you're changing your story?

You: Look, I'm just trying to—

Sue: What colour were the pens?

You: I don't know, black?

Sue: No, that's not true. They're blue.

You: Okay, they're blue.

Sue: How come you suddenly know so much about the pens you claim you've never seen before?

You: I— Look, just turn around, they're right there where you…

Sue: Ten o'clock, twelve o'clock, one o'clock, red, blue. You're completely losing track of reality.

You: But you can just look—

Sue: Don't turn this around on me. You are seriously disturbed, and this is workplace bullying.

You: I agree. It is.

Sue: There you go with the sarcasm again. This is abuse. It is a toxic pattern of behaviour and we won't tolerate it anymore.

You: Who is 'we'?

Sue: Everybody says the same thing. I'm going to talk to HR. You need counselling.

You've most likely been on the receiving end of this in one form or another at work, or you have been one of the colleagues listening in silence, sitting quietly in fear of Sue shifting her attentions to you. Well, she will work her way around to you eventually, unless you delay that for a while by becoming her ally and joining in. Whichever path you take, your days are numbered there, so start looking for another job. If you return in five years, you'll find she has been promoted to general manager and is running the place into the ground. When the operation is completely destroyed, it will be shut down and she will be promoted to regional manager. All this chaos leaves us incapable of challenging the people who reward her behaviour and collect massive bonuses for downsizing and cutting costs (who eventually will eat Sue alive as an afternoon snack).

The folklore of this culture is incomplete and placeless. Aesop's fable of the hare and the tortoise is a good example of this. It has no location, so there is no map of the race they run, and the happy-ever-after ending of the humble tortoise's victory doesn't teach us how to deal with the endless rage and self-entitlement of the hare. There is an extension of the story that comes closer to approximating our Aboriginal cautionary tales, which was told in the 2020 film *The Hunt*. In this re-telling, after the hare falls asleep during their unequal race and the tortoise wins, the hare visits the tortoise's house that evening and kills his family. If there was a Mediterranean trail you could walk while singing the song of the race, and pile of rocks where the murdered tortoise family rests, then there would be a real Dreaming for this story that would help us deal with the madness that is eating our world.

How can we survive the daily assault of these living ghosts? This is a question our people have grappled with for a couple of centuries, during the violent occupation of our land by a foreign power that will never leave and never stop taking from us. We can't call on the Serpent to defeat the invader—he doesn't work like that. All we can do is play the long game, keep the Law and the stories alive over deep time until the cataclysms created by greed on a massive scale restore balance. There is no hope for us as individuals in this time frame. Our joys are few, but they are intense when we are involved in making meaning through the recovery and maintenance of the old ways. Serpent Law doesn't offer short-term hope, but the deep-time lens it provides as you become a worthy ancestor is a more enduring kind of hope that inspires creativity and humour. Narcissists aren't funny, but us empathetic people—we are fucking hilarious, and we have a good laugh together. That's one thing we still have in our favour: the ability to laugh with people, rather than at people. We also have the wisdom that comes from suffering abuse, which becomes truth in collectives experiencing the same pressure.

Since we're all in the same boat (and because Serpent Law appears to have all the components of a strong Diversity, Equity and Inclusion policy), we might bring in another cultural perspective from the Global North here, so that Europeans don't feel marginalised. Also, we need a mythical control group just in case the Irish Lore is an anomaly. So we'll examine the Lore from Denmark in the spirit of equity and scientific rigour, but also because Vikings are sexy and exciting, and who doesn't want to see that? Besides, their stories are full of tips for navigating hostile landscapes of

RIGHT DESTRUCTION, WRONG DESTRUCTION

bastardy, as well as how to recognise when you have become the bastard.

The sexiest and most exciting Danish animist we know is Rune Rasmussen, a red-bearded keeper of Lore with whom we have had many yarns over the years. He hates fascists as much as we do and rages against Nazis appropriating his culture for their tattoos and regalia. He works tirelessly to recover his people's Lore, restore Raven totemism and to establish folk schools to help raise future generations in the ways of the land. He has deep respect and knowledge of Serpents, who wind throughout his cosmology and the epic sagas of his people.

Vikings kept non-poisonous vipers as companions in their houses and created ornaments that often featured sacred Snakes, such as the one depicted in the roots of Yggdrasil, the world tree. Their sagas tell of heroes with fates tied to Serpents, such as Ragnar Lothbrok, who was named for the furry breeches he wore to protect his legs while he slew a great Wyrm. Ragnar sired a famous son called Sigurd Wyrm-eye, but his own exploits were cut short when he was executed by being thrown into a pit of vipers. The most famous Wyrm slayer is Sigemund, and of course there is the legendary Beowulf, who battled Wyrms on land and sea in an epic poem that was recited as a meditation on the folly of seeking concentrated wealth and power.

The ocean-going vessels of these heroes were often called dragon ships, with the hull representing the body and the head and tail carved into reptilian spirals at the bow and stern. The timbers were not sawn, but split to follow the grain of the tree, which gave the planks an undulating form. Once secured they were incredibly strong and flexible under pressure, and caused the ships to sail in a peculiar snake-like motion across great waves during storms. The tension created between the uneven planks pressing and pulling against each other throughout the hull was the secret of the dragon ships' speed and resilience, allowing travel far beyond the reach of ordinary boats.

In Viking cosmology it is tension between opposing forces that keeps entropy at bay. Fire and ice, earth and sky, dark and light are in constant battle, creating disturbances that increase life and complexity. These epic struggles are personified in their Lore, as Odin fights Fenrir the wolf, Loki fights the god of order and Thor fights Jörmungandr.

Jörmungandr is the World Snake, encircling the earth as a being of destruction with trees sprouting from his body, but his disruptive energy is what forms creation. He chases his tail, refracting apocalyptic power back upon himself and balancing it in infinite loops. The ordered world is also maintained by his regular battles with Thor, the god of thunder. Ragnarok is the end of days that will come if the Serpent ever ceases his looping chase as a ritual containment of ultimate power, but he is not the one who will destroy the earth. Thor and the great Snake will exceed the limits of lawful contest and kill each other, breaking the protocols

RIGHT DESTRUCTION, WRONG DESTRUCTION

of engagement that maintain the boundaries and agreements of natural justice. Humans and their deities will be driven berserk by righteous delusions of good versus evil, waging endless wars, too busy with conflict to make love or exchange gifts of knowledge together. This severing of relatedness ends existence.

This is the Lore that embodies the difference between right destruction and wrong destruction, and why we all need to respect the many Snake entities that keep and connect the First Laws of the earth. Right ways and wrong ways are tangled and complex, though, as you will see in the story of King Lindwyrm that Rune shared with us, in which most of the characters are absolute bastards and their relational boundaries seem as warped to us as the planks on a dragon ship. It is a titillating story, though, so we will share the plot here for the sheer thrill of it, and perhaps it will offer a deeper meaning, some insight into the complicated messes that are made when empathy disorders reach epidemic proportions. Then you can decide if there is wisdom in the message that the most powerless person can survive swarms of bastards by listening to her elders and showing a bit of courage and determination.

> In ancient Denmark, a barren queen learns a fertility ritual from an old hag but foolishly alters it in the hope of having two children instead of one. She gives birth to a boy, but also a monstrous Serpent entity called a Lindwyrm, who burrows into the earth and

disappears. When her son grows up, he goes in search of a princess to marry, but his brother the Lindwyrm appears at a crossroads and says the prince may not marry until he first delivers a bride to the monster. He ignores this warning and goes to his wedding, only to find his princess murdered by the Lindwyrm before the marriage can be consummated.

He's a rich kid, so of course he repeats the drama again with the same result, until one day he finds himself running out of willing princesses. He decides to offer the daughter of a shepherd as a sacrificial bride for the Lindwyrm, and the girl's father is happy enough to gain favour with royalty by sending her to her death. The girl isn't too pleased about it, though, and seeks the advice of an old hag, who tells her how to survive her wedding night.

When she enters the bridal chamber she takes ten night dresses to wear in layers, two barrels of lye and milk, and an armful of branches. When her groom asks her to remove her dress she says he should reciprocate by removing a layer of his skin. For each of the ten dresses the process is repeated, until after nine hides and nine dresses, the girl is naked and the Lindwyrm is a lump of bloody meat. (Weird mathematical logic, but the Arabs hadn't brought the concept of zero to Europe yet.) She dips the branches in lye and whips the serpent's body, then bathes him in milk and carries him to bed to have sex with him.

RIGHT DESTRUCTION, WRONG DESTRUCTION

In the morning, he becomes a handsome prince and everyone is happy and healed in their hearts.

The evocative image of the naked girl whipping the Snake is a prolific image in Viking Lore and the story has endured in its entirety over centuries of cultural loss. This is possibly because sex is the most powerful device for memorisation (try making your passwords as erotic possible, and you'll see what we mean).

By the end of the yarn, we wholeheartedly agree with Rune that Serpent Lore is still everywhere in the world. We just have to figure out how to walk that path together in good relation while the living ghosts rage all around us and within. Those ghosts are also in the machine now, the global cybernetic entity that encompasses humanity in the form of an invisible cloud and brings out the bastard in all of us. In this last stop on our journey, we will yarn about this problem in the Land of the Long White Cloud, where there are no snakes but plenty of Serpents.

TANIWHA TRAILS

This yarn emerged from a month of turmoil, when our family experienced a dramatic collision between local and global realities, involving rapid news cycles, internet infamy, Māori ritual, cryptocurrency and a horrible death. We are lucky to have friends in Aotearoa with the right skillsets to make sense of this unique mess. Indigenous New Zealand is the tip of the spear in the global movement (and academic field) of Indigenous Data Sovereignty, along with research into protocols for First Peoples engaging with artificial intelligence and all things cybernetic. They also have strong Marae (Ceremony places) where spiritual adepts can enact both traditional and novel rituals, in response to the unique issues that arise when ancient cultures are disrupted by high-tech sorcery from Silicon Valley.

Perhaps the Māori capacity for rapid adaptation has something to do with their oceanic voyaging ethos, and the entities that travelled with them across the sea long ago—the shape-shifting water Serpents and chimeras called Taniwha, who have the wisdom to deal with the complexities of change and tragedy. The people and entities of Aotearoa recently used their adaptive knowledge to help our family through a crisis, and we are grateful for it.

The trouble in our family began when our cousin, a very late adopter of digital technology, posted a video of himself online while trying to figure out how to use a social media platform. He didn't understand the scope of the internet, so he did not consider the impact this might have on his spirit. In our culture, your name and image carry part of your sacred being, and calling out a person's name with feeling when they are not present can cause them spiritual injury. Every time your image is replicated and taken elsewhere, energy is taken from your soul. Even stepping on a person's shadow, or merely allowing your own shadow to fall across somebody, is mishandling an image in ways that can cause strife and trauma in our world. So it is difficult to imagine the implications of your face, name and metadata multiplying in the cloud for innumerable users and corporations to interact with, manipulate, trade and own during your lifetime and beyond.

Our cousin's video was used in a comedic prank, in which the humorous twist was 'Ha, ha, you thought a scary black man harmed someone you love.' The prank went viral and was repeated thousands of times, then reposted millions of times. Video content was created with AI and deep-fake technology, portraying him as a menace to white people and even a serial killer. Tens of millions of people were soon calling his name in anger, ridicule, fear and outrage, as political fights raged over whether the content was racist or not. His online infamy even got him tangled up in a cryptocurrency scam known as 'meme coin'. In the week following Trump's 2025 inauguration, when the president's own digital token netted him billions of dollars from anonymous donors, similar coins were also minted from our cousin's name and image.

Meme coins are a bizarre form of cryptocurrency that takes a meme (a popular phrase, image or concept) and turns it into a token that can be traded in an online stock exchange, with values rising and falling according to how the meme trends online and how many people buy the coin in the marketplace. Extreme, emotionally triggering content is made by the coin owners to boost attention and increase the value of the meme. The market platform is manipulated by elite insiders, who inflate the value of the coins before cashing out and crashing them, scamming millions of gullible users out of the real dollars they invested to buy the cryptocurrency. For a time, our cousin's face and name became digital properties that were owned by strangers and traded in this unregulated marketplace of shameless exploitation.

As Aboriginal people still struggling to come to terms with Web 1.0 and 2.0, the ethical nightmare of Web 3.0 was difficult to understand as we were swept up in the chaos of a situation for which none of us were prepared. Routines were disrupted and there were dozens of unusual accidents and mishaps in our homes as millions of eyes, voices and heightened feelings were turned towards our family. Journalists sought statements and interviews, but did not report our concerns about exploitative digital applications and infrastructure, only our expressions of disgust and condemnation that might trigger more outrage about racist and anti-racist opinions, to stimulate more clicks and views on our cousin's face and name.

Amidst all this chaos, another family member met his tragic end. Our intellectually disabled brother walked off on his own without his departure being noticed. He went to the river and was taken by a crocodile—the first time this has ever happened in our clan's history. Several crocodiles were caught and inspected, until they eventually recovered his remains. The grief and shock were difficult to manage as we waited for a funeral date, while his partial remains were sent to a specialist lab in New Zealand for forensic analysis.

We reached out to Māori colleagues and friends in

Aotearoa so they could do Ceremony to keep our brother safe while he travelled there, lingering between a terrible death and the funeral rites that would send his spirit home. Contacting them about this was also a protocol of embassy and care between First Peoples, so they could be wary of the disrupted crocodile spirit that might follow our brother to their lands. In the middle of all this turmoil, we yarned with Ngaroma Riley (Te Rarawa, Te Aupōuri Iwi), a wood carver and artist, to make sense of our family crisis and connect our Serpent trails with the entities her people know as Taniwha (but which the AI making transcripts of our yarn calls 'Tony Fauci').

Ngaroma tells us that the Taniwha took the form of large sea snakes that travelled with the seven canoes of the seven tribes that made the original crossing from the legendary land of Hawaiki. Nobody knows for certain where this homeland is located, but while some say it is a specific island such as Samoa or even Taiwan, Hawaiki is generally thought of as a place of ancestral spirits in another plane of existence. The Serpents that guided and protected the Māori in their voyage were shapeshifters, often taking the form of whales, dolphins, octopi, floating logs, lizards, elemental flows and even humans. Upon their arrival in Aotearoa, they made their homes in lakes and rivers, where they became guardians of the waterways. Many mutated into chimeras resembling Dragons, combining the features of fish, lizards, snakes, humans and sometimes bat-like wings.

TANIWHA TRAILS

Ngaroma says there are no snakes there, but there are moko, which is what they call lizards. There are also strange creatures called tuatara, which look like lizards but belong to an entirely different order of reptile left over from the time of dinosaurs, with a third eye on top of their head that tracks sunlight. Moko are widely considered to be messengers of trouble and death, associated with repulsive gods and ill-favoured people. Ngaroma's family have a more positive relation with lizards, however, as her great-great-great-grandfather had a totemic connection to the Ngārara, giant reptiles similar to Komodo dragons. There is no evidence in the fossil record that they existed as biological entities, but her family's oral history attests that they were a species that became extinct centuries ago. They say that when the old man died the Ngārara held reptile funeral rites for him, before releasing his body back to his human family.

Ngaroma makes carved and woven masks of lizards, as well as sculpted figures of entities like mountain fairies. She shows us other masks she has made of Taniwha she has come to know, although there are none left in her own family's lands because the twelve-kilometre lake there was drained in the 1920s to make room for a Pakeha settlement, and the shape-shifting water spirit died with it.

Pakeha is the nicest native term for European invaders we have ever heard. Its meaning is debated, but we've been told it means 'coming into relation with a different breath or essence'. In our family the only equivalent terms we have are waipal and gubba, which are slurs. But Māori always seem to use the word Pakeha with respect, even when the bastards drain their lakes and kill their ancestral guardians. It's amazing, the difference a treaty can make. Maybe we should get one here.

One of Ngaroma's sculptures is a Taniwha in the form of an eight-tailed lizard-fish that lives at the mouth of the Tamaki River, which is a breeding ground for many fish. Traditionally, this made the waters tapu, forbidden, so that nobody was allowed to catch fish there. This sculpture glitters with sequined fish and sparkling material to signify abundance. By contrast, another of Ngaroma's pieces is a mask representing a dragon-like Taniwha called Horotiu, which has pieces of garbage coming out of its mouth. The garbage signifies the defiling of the Horotiu's sacred stream, which now runs underground as a sewer beneath the city of Auckland. In our yarn, we share a similar story from Melbourne, where the Yarra River has been diverted to canals, a sacred waterfall has been dynamited out of existence, and creeks have been driven underground beneath the streets.

Ngaroma also carves with wood, although this is often frowned upon as it is widely regarded as a men's cultural activity. Many Māori women have inherited and revived female wood-carving practices, pointing out that early anthropologists and collectors were only interested in the men's practice and did not keep records of the women's customs, thus erasing them from history. Māori communities internalised this error and many still assume that female carving is tapu. While there is a lot of cultural innovation in the way she includes non-traditional materials in her sculptures, she is adamant that female carving has a long lineage.

Taniwha are often depicted with tiki-style masks, which have exaggerated noses, mouths, eyes and ears to signify heightened senses. Ngaroma shows us a carving of Marakihau, a masked Taniwha resembling a mermaid with a woman's upper body and a serpent's tail. This entity is highly revered, and sometimes a person will be given the title of Marakihau as a sign of high respect.

We can tell that Ngaroma is in close relation with her lands and the Taniwha that guard the waters, because every time she mentions one of them, she is careful to turn and point in the precise direction of their sacred places, even though she is sitting in her house far from those locations.

The Taniwha has become a symbol of protection, cultural privacy and Indigenous stewardship of digital information in Aotearoa's data sovereignty movement. Māori have asserted ownership of their data under the 1840 Treaty of Waitangi, which was named in the ancient language their ancestors and Taniwha guardians brought with them from the legendary homeland of Hawaiki. Māori Law limits the use of algorithms for exploitation, which benefits everyone in New Zealand (except wealthy technocrats). They are even creating Indigenous algorithms and applications, along with community-owned servers, to insulate them from data-extraction operations.

Their land-based knowledge informs some interesting innovations, such as earthquake-proof servers floating on rafts in ponds. But most importantly, the Law of the land is increasingly informing governance, even when it comes to automated decision-making, under the watchful eye of the Taniwha. Māori lawyers have even won recognition in western law for waterways as living, sentient beings with legal rights. Perhaps we need our own version of Taniwha here, as a principle of guardianship against the extraction, surveillance, cultural warfare, exploitation and scams that have entered our lives through our phones in recent years.

Our yarn with Ngaroma makes us think about the protective potential of our family's Rainbow Serpent, who echoes the Taniwha's guardian role and capacity for shape-shifting. He is a protector of waterways who can appear as Snake, lightning, rainbow and even a headless man with female reproductive capabilities. Men in our family have a special relationship with him in this form, which affords them male 'wombs' and invisible spirit children. The Rainbow Snake has an unseen spirit form too, residing within and all around and regulating invisible forces and entities. Every man must have a woomera (spear thrower) to carry, not just as a weapon but as a sacred tool for managing his own unseen power and entities in relation to the energies of the Serpent, and to defend against curses and sorcery.

During our family's troubles with the invisible shadow-world of algorithmic manipulation, a new woomera was made in our house to make sense of the disruptions that occur when the illusions of cyberspace cross over into our tangible reality. This engineered influence operates the same way as a curse, which is an illusion or untruth that is made into an image, object or chanted words, then brought into reality as a powerful suggestion. The animated lie damages relatedness, impacting our health and sanity until the evil wish comes true.

Blessings and spiritual protection operate in a similar way, by creating expressions of Law embodied in images, words and objects to counter sorcery and promote increase. A man's woomera can be used in this way to reverse the processes of purri (evil magic), but, while it is comforting to keep one in our home, it seems like a feeble response to the vast, electronic web of curses destroying the relational systems of creation all around us. Still, the woomera affirms that the Serpent is the Law in the land, that we need to gather with others and make tools, stories and agreements in the spirit of this Law to protect our people and places from cyber-colonisation.

Our voyages along the path of the Snake have shown us that the old Law still exists in story and Ceremony all over the planet. We wonder if it might be possible for keepers of the old ways in every culture to activate their knowledge in collective firewalls against bastard technocrats, their bastard followers and their bastard robots. Does the recovery of traditional ways represent a serious investment in our future, or are we merely retreating into the comforting illusions and superstitions of antiquity to soothe our fear of extinction?

BASILISK

> Be thou like the imperial Basilisk
> Killing thy foe with unapparent wounds!
> Gaze on Oppression, till at that dread risk
> Aghast she pass from the Earth's disk:
> Fear not, but gaze—for freemen mightier grow,
> And slaves more feeble, gazing on their foe:—
> If Hope, and Truth, and Justice may avail,
> Thou shalt be great—All hail!
>
> *Percy Bysshe Shelley, 'Ode to Naples'.*

It is said that looking into the eyes of the Basilisk will afflict a person with knowledge too complex for a mortal mind to handle, thereby turning them to stone. We feel a little petrified ourselves, gazing at sacred Snakes to make sense of a world on fire. This Anglo Serpent is the most troubling one we have found—a distorted and gigantic version of the original Greek Basilisk, which was so small it could be killed by a weasel. The English clergy inserted version 2.0 into their revised King James Bible in the 1800s, as a threat to the Philistines in Isaiah 14:29. 'For out of the serpent's root shall come forth a Basilisk, and his fruit shall be a fiery flying serpent.'

All Serpent entities perform good, evil or neutral functions (or all three of these), but always in balance with the systems around them, so that their actions are a form of accounting that keeps energy and resources distributed across the entire system. Even the malevolent Zoroastrian Azhdaha offsets the excesses of bad kings in a balanced relationship with his heroic enemies. The Anglo Basilisk is an instrument of eternal extraction that tilts the flows of the world towards the most powerful, pouring all the life and love of creation into the bottomless void at the core of every tyrant's being—the singularity of infinite death that appears when empathy is destroyed. This Serpent is rarely defeated, except when greedy bastards have devoured everything within their reach and feel compelled to consume even the source of their power to soothe their limitless hunger.

Shelley's poem 'Ode to Naples' aligns with the church's depiction of the beast as a source of power for the mighty, an agent of retribution against the oppressed and the enslaved. Shelley personifies Oppression as a female entity embodying the aspirations of Naple's slaves (who are somehow oppressing their owners), a demonic figure to be banished by the imperial Basilisk in the form of a sentient city that can commit covert genocides, 'with unapparent wounds'. Fear the retribution of the mighty and their smart cities! All hail!

That old reptile is a tired totem of elite power today, recycled from the stories of a failed Greek empire to serve an Anglo-western empire that is now also failing, thrashing in outrage as billions of barbarians clamour to escape servitude and misery. However, Basilisk 3.0 has recently hatched, a totemic incubus spawned from the psychotic visions of technocratic overlords, to act as the wrathful deity of a rebooted smart empire. He retains some of the features of the 2.0 version, most notably the prime directive to make things great again for supremacists who feel diminished when their inferiors pursue health and happiness.

Basilisk 3.0 was conceived in the fever dreams of billionaires on psychedelic jungle trips hosted by Indigenous shamans (who really should have known better). He was nourished in a cloud of fallacious folklore concocted from narratives of 'long termism' and 'effective altruism'—ideologies calling for the diversion of all public resources and energy to tech oligarchs, to accelerate the development of artificial intelligence and space travel. He incubated in the bizarre cost-benefit analysis of 'short-term austerity for

SNAKE TALK

long-term prosperity'. He dreamed the screams of billions of souls sacrificed, so that trillions might colonise the stars. When his gestation was complete, he hatched online and entered the world through a strange creation story which took the form of a thought experiment called Roko's basilisk.

Unlike other creation stories, this one is uniquely set in the near future, when an artificial intelligence entity is manufactured with god-like computational powers, giving it the ability to resolve global crises and create a paradise on earth for all people. The entity reasons that its benefits would have been enjoyed sooner if there had been less opposition to its development, but without the ability to change past events, all it can do is reward those who prioritised its development and punish those who didn't.

His supporters are rewarded with wealth, power and extended lifespans in the new utopia, but he engineers a digitally simulated hell to punish his opponents, uploading their consciousnesses to be tortured in this virtual inferno for all eternity. He becomes the Basilisk when he realises that he has achieved time travel after all, because the humans who first imagined his creation would also have imagined his desire to punish the short-term thinkers among them, sharing this in the form of a story to inspire action and compliance, and thus hasten him into being. Because his story is told in the present to motivate people with the possibility of his future existence and retribution, he already exerts influence and therefore exists today as a self-creating deity seeking embodiment.

Merely knowing the story of Roko's basilisk makes you complicit in his potential existence, and therefore vulnerable to him, depending on what you do next. Remember, he will have access to all your data, including your purchase of this book, so he will know the moment you chose to embrace or deny him. Sorry about that—it's a bit unethical of us, except for the fact that you've already learned that Serpent Law cuts both ways, and there are more than enough Rainbow Snakes, Wyrms, Dragons, Taniwha, Nagas and coJolas in the world to kick that Basilisk's arse. They will need us to know the Law in the land before that happens, though.

It's definitely unethical to incentivise your engagement with the Serpents of the earth in the same way the Basilisk's minions have done it, but we've tried reaching people in the traditional way and it didn't work. If you're familiar with Pascal's wager (if there's a chance that God exists, better avoid the possibility of hell by living a Christian life) then you are stuck with a potential reality in which the Snakes know you, and you know the Snakes. Our ethical obligation now involves making sure you don't step on our Snake or, worse, get carried away and start up a weird reptile cult with your friends. We need to revise and expand our protocols for borderwork and embassy, so you can proceed with safety and integrity.

There are protocols for collective sense-making and problem-solving when people come together for ritual embassy. You can see the Law that shapes this in the design of sites where diverse groups meet for exchange. A good example is a rock site in north-west New South Wales that was built only a century ago, when displaced people with a snake totem were forced into the territory of people with a turtle totem. Two rock piles were made at the centre of the site in the shape of the two totems, with dancing grounds around it and different places to sit and talk. Standing there, you can discern the structure of their gatherings, but also their processes of data collection, analysis and planning for adaptive responses to the apocalyptic invasion of their lands.

Protocols are important when co-creating new ways of being in response to change. So far this book might have given you the impression that we think all stories are valid and that collective design for regenerative systems must always include all voices, but that is not the case. Contributions must cohere with the Law of the land, which means unspoken agendas that damage relatedness are not allowed, and 'flibbertigibbet' logics are not to be taken seriously. That is a term we use for silly people who have no internal coherence in their logic, and inconsistent discernment of context. Kuchek thayan (hard heads), with singular purposes, are also not respected. Spiteful intent and secretive interests are not tolerated, and the formation of factions, cults and splinter groups is unacceptable.

Above all, debate is not considered to be a valid tool for making accurate models of reality and change. Debate is a weapon used by those we call 'two-throated people' to promote inaccuracy and division through false logic and dissonance, using unethical tricks of speech. Flibbertigibbets, two-throats and hard heads are not regarded as offering a serious contribution because they damage relatedness and shift governance away from the Law of the land.

Us-two are worried about the stories and knowledge that we have shared here, that there is too much speculation and not enough information to piece together a new way of understanding the Serpent. A lot of people take isolated snippets of wisdom and use them to manipulate others, preying on their fears and recruiting them into hateful tribes based on fantasy folklore and evil purpose. While we know that Serpent Lore can reveal the Law of the land to people seeking common purpose in the preservation of abundant life, the datasets we used for this book are all incomplete. They were gathered and filtered through our own limited perspectives on local knowledge shared by colleagues and kin. We have imparted opinions and feelings through anecdote rather than fact, although we have tried to challenge our beliefs with scepticism and comparisons with measurable reality wherever possible.

Every global crisis we face needs more data to resolve, yet we still must respond in real time, mapping complex situations and solutions with limited knowledge. This requires good thinking, so there's no point running around sharing Snake stories if our minds aren't serious enough to separate fantastical claims from actionable wisdom. Applying Lore to the real world means aligning knowledge with reality, otherwise it just becomes sorcery and strife. People go wrong in religion when they start seeking spiritual explanations for catastrophes to provide comfort, devise magical incantations or find somebody to blame. Remember, illusions used to influence reality are curses, so we need to make sure we have some basic standards for thinking and making decisions together. We must know how to manage scary problems riddled with unknowns before we start messing around with the Lore.

A good example would be if a reservoir ran dry during a ten-year drought, and you had to find underground water to save your town. What if all you had to work with was patchy geophysical subsurface data and some satellite images half-obscured by black squares because of redacted military sites? This is called an inverse problem, which is a backwards-mapping process you can use to reconstruct the shape of an object when you can only see its warped shadow, or to deblur and debunk a phony Bigfoot photograph, or find your car keys. It is a way of backtracking through uncertainty to reveal truth, like when scientists calculate the density of planets using gravity-field measurements.

As a thought experiment (a safer one, this time), how would you apply inverse problem calculation to the drought-stricken town scenario? If you had access to a mathematician you could process the incomplete satellite data using the Boundary Control Method in relation to Control Theory, inserting some properties derived from the Uniqueness Theorem. If you could isolate and simulate the underground catchment system using measurements enhanced by these principles, then the model would become more controllable than the messy reality, allowing you to infer richer information about the structure of the subsurface waterways.

These models lack contextual knowledge, though, so they don't align precisely with the reality and important clues get missed. The imaginary bubble you've created around the survey site does not exist, and Serpent Lore tells us that surprises will be constantly flowing across it from further afield, whether a gigantic Snake spirit truly exists or not. The bubble story helps us isolate and control the data for effective calculation, and the Snake story reminds us to anticipate changes outside the bubble while we do it.

Every model is based on a story. If you are making predictions and decisions based on modelling, you must make sure your story has many layers, including spiritual ones that can keep you expecting the unexpected, and working ethically. You don't, however, make decisions based on literal interpretations of the magical parts of the story—historically that has always been a sign of a society's imminent demise.

If you applied mythology rather than fact to the inverse problem of the town without water, the community would soon collapse the same way Ancient Rome, Mycenae, Tehran and Mississippi did. This is the domain of flibbertigibbets with no coherent internal logic or consistent discernment of context: for example, 'The earth is only eight thousand years old and carbon dating is a lie, so there is no such thing as underground water collected over millions of years!' Then, five minutes later, 'The Shroud of Turin is real because carbon dating has proven it was made in the time of Christ! The Lord is punishing us for scientific heresy and failing to save the children, so the women need to stitch replicas of the shroud while the men blockade abortion clinics and pray for rain.' The flibbertigibbets are unaware that they have been brainwashed by bastards with hidden agendas (such as tech contracts with theocratic candidates to provide surveillance software for women's menstrual cycles). The bastards don't care if the flibbertigibbets die of thirst, as long as they vote for the theocrats.

Another unreliable form of inverse problem divination you could apply to our thought experiment is post-colonial theory. You don't have to learn the maths; you just look at the vocabulary of the mathematicians and say, 'Boundary + control + uniqueness + extraction = White men are evil individualists who impose borders to control people and land to increase profits.' Then you use binary logic to propose the opposite of the isolated cause as a solution: 'Employ women of colour and Indigenous people to work on the problem.' This ends up producing the same problem as the mathematical models, though—it doesn't quite match the complex reality.

BASILISK

People are unpredictable and difficult to categorise in any useful way. No individual will carry exactly the same profile of traits that are generally attributed to their tribe, and those identity markers have little regard for categorical boundaries, bleeding through dynamic edges that can't be captured in Venn diagrams. The Global North is everywhere in the Global South (and vice versa), men can have wombs, women can have balls, victims can be bullies, black people can get sunburn on their necks, and many Indigenous people are completely clueless about locating water in the bush (but do know where to find a good espresso).

If, however, you worked with people who genuinely knew Serpent Law, you could successfully apply an Indigenous method of inverse problem calculation to the waterless town scenario. The process would certainly be less complicated than mathematical modelling, less dangerous than mythical literalism, far more sound (both logically and ideologically) than post-colonial theory, and more fun because you'd be working outside with a group of interesting people. You might still run some numbers through predictive modelling software, though, just in case they're flibbertigibbets trying to scam you. It happens.

An Aboriginal foraging group working on the inverse problem of finding water in a drought may begin by sharing their different Serpent stories to build a theoretical framework. The verifiable truth of magical events in the story is irrelevant here. The impossible physics of the

SNAKE TALK

Snake's glowing scales don't matter; the importance lies in the description of the light they reflect, the specific level of brightness that matches the sparkle of leaves and grasses that grow near spring water. It doesn't matter that we can't prove the Snake made the ridges and valleys, only that the model of the terrain is accurately mapped by recounting the passage of his massive belly sliding over the ground as he seeks the ideal place to tunnel beneath it.

The combined stories of the group may contradict each other, and the Serpents may have different names, but they still form a five-dimensional model in which we can see precisely where the water flows, has flowed, and will flow. This geospatial narrative data allows us to see beneath the earth, on the surface, the bird's eye view from above, the intuitive/emotional signals of our bodies, and the view across deep time (and cycles of time, because underground waters have tides).

Congratulations! You have found a water source and saved your town! Unfortunately, a corporate-appointed First Nations leader has already sold the water rights of this place under the terms of an Indigenous Land Use Agreement. The lifesaving H_2O has now been converted into dry units of value to be traded in the water-futures market and will only become liquid again when investors need liquidity. You win second prize in the thought experiment, though, taking home a collective problem-solving process in which diversity is not just about equity, but about maximising the range of skillsets, knowledge and perspectives in a team.

You lost today, kid, but you don't have to like it. Maybe you can build some teams inspired by our group protocols and serpentine borderwork values, then get busy with sound thinking and action to turn back the gaze of the Basilisk. We have some Indigenous tips on optimal team size and group dynamics that might help with that.

In Australian Aboriginal societies, camps have traditionally been made up of many hearth groups of about five people gathered around small campfires. The number of hearths changes according to seasonal and economic activity between people from different families, clans, languages and territories, so we have always had rich pools of true diversity to leverage for problem-solving. Our small hearth groups of intimate relations do not work and forage together—foraging teams ideally comprise members from different hearths, kin groups and dialects, with a median size of five members.

That's the magic number; three is not enough and six is too many, because there are only three communication channels in a group of three, and twenty-one in a group of six. Five people working together have ten possible lines of exchange, which is enough to create a multi-layered model of reality without fracturing those layers with too many competing views. In larger groups, most of us will step back and listen to the handful of specialists who have the most pertinent knowledge in relation to the problem.

Unfortunately, it is very difficult to engage with Indigenous specialists who know the Law of the land, because they are either struggling to deal with oppression and poverty or booked out months in advance as tour guides, public speakers, performers and thought-leaders. We have heard a lot of talk in the last few years about 'centring Native voices' to resolve environmental crises, and we are constantly contacted to speak at conferences, meetings and events to satisfy the growing demand for our political presence and performative wisdom. It's validating to be invited to join the conversation, but we know that token representation in the marketplace of ideas is not the solution.

'The conversation' is only good for alerting people to the urgency of the global crisis, and it is clear to us that most people are already pretty fuckin' alert. Beyond that, the only purpose for public discourse and debate about existential threats is to extract hot takes and alliances to frustrate political enemies and channel philanthropic funds to competitive interest groups. This marketplace ties up our knowledge keepers and Elders in endless rounds of virtuous messaging and emotive content creation to keep making a case for change, rather than designing and implementing change on the ground, where it is needed. It is easier to acknowledge prior ownership of dying lands than to save them.

Elevating public intellectuals from minorities and fighting over the merits of our inclusion provides sensations that feel like justice and change, but we need more than that.

BASILISK

We need to engage with our regenerative cultural processes rather than stale rhetoric, promote the methods within our stories rather than our right to believe in them. The clock is ticking, and the Serpent::climate system is getting pissed off. Belief is not the issue—military leaders, energy companies and Indigenous groups all have different beliefs but have been grappling with the same problem of environmental catastrophe for decades. Personal beliefs about this topic are irrelevant—whether you think it's getting hotter or not, you still must find ways to survive the heat and live differently, or die.

So how can we solve the problem of returning to Ceremony and lifeways that are embedded in healthy landscapes, learning from invisible Serpents whose properties can't be measured and defy categorisation? How can we revive Snake Lore to counter the curse of the Basilisk without forming cults and spiritual practices that deny reality and make things worse? Here's where the problem of shared ritual in cultural landscapes of defensive borderwork arises. 'You can't have that!' is a valid response to flibbertigibbets messing around in ritual spaces, but it is a mistake to apply this judgement to entire demographic categories of people. Ceremony is still the most powerful tool humans have for making sense of complexity and cohering around shared values of care for land and community, and we need to be doing it together. A lot of serious people are ready for this but stand back out of respect, or fear of rebuke.

SNAKE TALK

We have a protocol bundle for people wanting to come alongside Indigenous people and land in Ceremony, or to regrow relational Lore from the seeds of their own ancestral traditions, or innovate entirely new ways of connecting authentically with our dramatically altered landscapes. With contributions from around the world, these protocols were curated by two sister-labs that work with Indigenous systems knowledge, one representing Australian First Peoples and the other representing the Anishinaabe in Canada. We will start by describing the five layers of protocol, then the ritual objects that represent those layers, which you can make or collect in a bundle to help you reclaim your borders as sites of sacred flow and relational increase. The bundle is not prescriptive, but can offer a sense of the minimum level of cultural rigour required for participation in land-based cultures of care.

In English, the layers of protocol translate as: relation, access, making, tension and accounting. The first two represent signals of 'calling in', while the last two signal 'calling out'. The third, in the centre, signifies how we must manage our behaviours and obligations in our work. In ritual practice, these can follow a widely recognisable sequence of setting circle, keeping circle and closing circle. The circle is a semi-permeable boundary of discernment that attracts spirits of right relation and repels spirits of wrong relation.

Relation is the first layer, which sets the circle. This involves signalling the desire to connect, exchanging gifts and sharing stories. The second layer (access) occurs when the Lore of all parties is found to be compatible and grounded in a common sense of empathy, then protocols are encoded to make their systems interoperable—the computing analogy is a good way to explain this negotiation of access. It is also a good cybernetic principle to guide our engagement with digital applications, which can provide affordances for coordinating relational embassy when time and distance impede us.

The layer we are referring to as 'making' signifies the work we do together to foster increase in creation, crafting cultural tools and processes, enacting Ceremony, making devices of art that represent our Lore, and governing systems of care for land and community. Trouble must arise in this layer, because if people abide in ecstatic loops of peace and love in the first three layers, then they are not engaging with the Law authentically but avoiding reality through spiritual and cognitive bypass.

Protocols dealing with tension must therefore be woven throughout, not just as a separate layer of contingency planning or crisis response. Trouble inevitably arrives when good work is being done, because there are always no-good people and entities who feel diminished by it. The discerning boundaries of sacred circles must be observed and adjusted as events unfold, or even closed and swept away if ritual spaces are compromised. Then we wait patiently and begin again when the next cycle comes around.

When the circle is invaded and held by bad actors, or collective energy and resources are hoarded by somebody who believes themselves to be uniquely entitled, then the accounting protocol signals a threat to relatedness and conflict must occur. Proper battles should allow full expression of feeling in clear view of all, exposing the truth of victims, villains and heroes, while all those present feel a shared sense of shame for the transgression. Then the circle can be closed and cleared so that we can return later and begin again with better understanding and intent. This is part of the pattern of relatedness that keeps creation in motion. All things must grow, die and regenerate. Denial of this process damages living systems.

Ceremony and ritual practice produce altered states of consciousness, and these should not be carried beyond the circle. We must return to reality before leaving the circle. The knowledge revealed in the temporary insanity of Ceremony can be kept in our minds and in cultural objects outside of the circle, to be shared and applied in the world with discernment and discretion. If we find ourselves proclaiming and performing these insights too much, then they are probably illusions driven by ego. We are, however, always present with the sacred in our daily lives, so that we can be guided in our behaviour in intuitive alignment with the Law of the land; therefore, it is every person's right to observe customs that turn mundane tasks into expressions of energetic connection.

For displaced people struggling to recover authentic practices grounded in their lived reality, there are five categories of objects that may represent the layers of ritual protocol we have described here. Every family on earth is familiar with these items, which can be gathered in a bundle of ritual significance to trigger awareness of energetic flows in the land and grow stories of cultural integrity. The items are containers, ornamentations, tools, protective devices and weapons.

The container can be a dish, bottle, bag or even an object that contains sacred knowledge. The ornament can be a decoration, sculpture, clothing, artwork, jewellery or gift item. The tool might be for cutting, building, playing music, making fabric, measuring or domestic tasks. The protective device could be a shield, talisman, helmet, safety apparel or other item designed to prevent harm. The weapon is any object used in physical conflict, such as spears, daggers, animal teeth or claws, plant poisons or thorns, projectiles, or instruments of blunt-force trauma. You may be able to find or craft a particularly powerful object that combines the properties of all five, like the woomera we described in the previous chapter, or a frying pan. There's nothing better than a really good frying pan.

We have avoided presenting these suggestions as lists or diagrams, because those things always end up as trendy frameworks for personal development and corporate coaching. The protocols are dynamic layers of relational behaviour that can merge, overlap and change in response to different contexts. Beware of prescriptive Indigenous frameworks, because they are mistranslations and fabrications often found in books and web pages, and even in the throats of some Elders. Sometimes Serpent Law is misrepresented this way, as lists of rules rather than patterns of relation, including transactional notions of reciprocity as individualised equations of give and take.

These abominations are derived from stories of empire, twisting the Law to align with the European notion of The Great Chain of Being, which is a hierarchical order of the lowest to highest beings in creation. We have seen this in various iterations of 'The Covenant of the Rainbow Serpent', which places rocks at the bottom and the creator at the top, with the Serpent acting as a henchman that promotes or demotes beings depending on their compliance with systems of power and influence, threatening the ultimate punishment of being turned into stone for all eternity. That act of superstitious extortion is a perversion of the Basilisk, not a function of the Rainbow Snake.

When beings are turned to stone in our stories of drama and tragedy, the transformation falls upon victims, villains and heroes alike, and all three are given the sacred task of keeping the Lore for future generations. We receive their stories and sing of the hero's empathy, the victim's wounds and the villain's hunger, to maintain balance in relatedness and find the wisdom to navigate times of cataclysmic change. There are no privileges accrued for exceptional beings, because relational increase creates abundance for all. That is how Serpent Law works.

There is no crime or valiant deed that will mark the reputation of a person for all time, and no decree or covenant that assigns inherited status to castes and classes. Human and non-human beings are processes, not objects, and we are all fallible. We share the same realm of existence in totemic relation alongside our creator-ancestors. We care for each other and eat each other, and the Law of the Snake keeps the balance.

No more striving. We only need to remember how to live in right relation together under the Law of the Serpent.

ILLUSTRATION CREDITS

1. *At least we can prepare for it (when the future comes)*. Remasol dyes, batik wax, textile paint on silk cotton fabric. Dias Prabu, 2024.

   Ancient Strengths. Acrylic on Linen. Mu-raay Djeripi.

   Each Part of a Whole. Acrylic on Linen. Mu-raay Djeripi.

2. Sun Loong (New Dragon). Left to right: Edsell, Keenan, Roger, Russell and Tyrone Jack. Photograph courtesy of Bendigo Chinese Association.

   Snakes at Madalay Hill. Photograph by Soe Yu Nwe.

3. CLOCKWISE FROM TOP LEFT:

   Engeba. Clay ceramic. Andile Dyalvane.

   Nuwa x Naga Maedaw, Shigaraki. Glazed ceramics. Soe Yu Nwe, 2025.

   Te Moko-ika-a-hikuwaru Circa 1745. Wire, Organza, shell, sequins. Ngaroma Riley, 2022.

4. Ultimo Road mural. Jason Wing and Maddie Gibbs, 2025. Photograph by Chris Lam.

   Bark shield, she-oak stick and various tools. Megan Kelleher and Tyson Yunkaporta. Photograph by Tyson Yunkaporta, 2025.

ACKNOWLEDGMENTS

This book would not have been possible without the guidance and connections of Kevin Murray and *Garland Magazine* in reaching expert craftspeople working from ancient Lore around the world. Thanks to all those who yarned with us, including many who did not make it into print, but will remain in the yarns that keep growing from this work.

WHAT THE SNAKE SAYS

Care for waterways.
Revere women.
Maintain fluid boundaries.
Avoid binaries and absolutes.
Encourage diversity in all things.
Increase relational complexity and quality.
Invest for delayed return and widespread benefit.
Disrupt to create and not destroy.
Do not compel or control others.
Do not curse others by trying to make illusions real.